FOR IMMEDIATE RELEASE

Also by Adrian A. Paradis

NEVER TOO YOUNG TO EARN:
101 Part Time Jobs for Girls

FOR IMMEDIATE RELEASE

Careers in Public Relations

by

ADRIAN A. PARADIS

DAVID McKAY COMPANY, INC.

NEW YORK

LIBRARY OF CONGRESS CATALOG CARD NO. 55-8998

Manufactured in the United States of America.

VAN REES PRESS • NEW YORK

Typography by Charles M. Todd

To Muriel Fuller

CONTENTS

PART 3

Your Public Relations Career

INTRODUCTION

THE PURPOSE of *For Immediate Release* is to take you by the hand and gently introduce you to the profession of Public Relations and a few of its practitioners. As we discuss Public Relations we shall point out how it serves mankind, explain the use of its principal tools, indicate the important qualifications for entering the profession, suggest how you may prepare for a public relations career, hint at some of the rewards you may expect to garner, and warn you of the pitfalls that can lie ahead.

If you are a young man or woman who is seriously thinking of your future and exploring with an open mind the possibilities of a number of careers, this book is intended for you. After reading *For Immediate Release*, you will know whether or not the public relations profession is of interest to you. If it is, the next step is to do something about it and you will find helpful suggestions in the last chapter and in Appendix A.

Should you decide that Public Relations is not for you, we believe that any information you absorb about the profession will prove useful on many occasions. No matter what business or professional career you ultimately choose, somewhere along the line you will find that even an *awareness* of the necessity for effective public relations will prove extremely helpful.

There is no activity or undertaking involving people that cannot benefit from some form of good public relations.

PART 1

UNDERSTANDING PUBLIC RELATIONS

CHAPTER

1

WHAT IS PUBLIC RELATIONS?

A TRAIN WAS speeding between Michigan City in Indiana and Chicago on October 8, 1882. In his luxurious private car William Henry Vanderbilt, president of the New York Central Railroad and son of the famous Commodore Vanderbilt, was entertaining a group of newspaper reporters. They were clamoring to know more about the rate war which had broken out between the New York Central and the Pennsylvania Railroad. Vanderbilt told them that his road could not make a profit on passengers who paid but fifteen dollars to travel from New York to Chicago and it was keeping the rate in effect simply because it was forced to do so by the Pennsylvania. Otherwise, he told them emphatically, the Central would have abandoned the fare.

When asked if the railroad was not run for the benefit of the public, Vanderbilt quickly replied: "The public be damned!" He was running the New York Central for the benefit of the stockholders.

Much progress has been made between the time Vanderbilt made his never-to-be-forgotten remark and today, when the science of public relations is conducted by experts, many of whom are professionally trained.

WHAT IS PUBLIC RELATIONS?

In its very broadest sense, public relations is dealing successfully with people. As such, it is part of the science of human relations. It is practiced by every man and woman, boy and girl, every day of the year. It is a powerful force for good in the home, at school, in the office or factory, in the street; in fact, wherever human beings meet or have some kind of contact. Obviously there are many kinds of public relations. They run the gamut from very good to very bad.

Our definition of public relations is not yet quite complete. If we say that public relations is dealing successfully with people, we imply that it is a selfish proposition designed to bring the user personal gain. If, on the other hand, we say that public relations is dealing successfully with people, *with the emphasis on an activity that is beneficial to the public* or *that endeavors to gain the good will and understanding of the public,* we have given it a real purpose and objective.

Having glorified public relations with this fine definition, let's hastily admit that every public relations program is motivated by a selfish desire to accomplish some purpose. It may strive merely to deal successfully with people by creating a good impression. It may not necessarily place emphasis on an activity that is beneficial to the public.

Few of us are aware of the needs that exist in our community for good public relations. Perhaps we may get a better understanding of just what public relations is if we consider how you and I are affected in our home town by the public relations programs of various groups.

"But," you say, "I live in a small town. I never heard of anyone conducting a public relations program."

All right. Remembering that public relations is the science

of dealing with people successfully and sometimes with benefit for the public, let's see just what does take place.

HOW IS YOUR PUBLIC RELATIONS POLICY?

Take yourself first, because there is no one whom you know better. You have never had a personal public relations program because obviously such an idea never entered your head. But are you a friendly individual? Do you meet people easily and is yours a warm personality? The manner in which you meet and deal with others is the outward expression of your subconscious public relations policy. Perhaps we might say that the way you treat people is determined by your personality, which might be called the director of your own public relations program.

Thus, if you are an extrovert, the type of person who bubbles over with exuberance, meets people easily, readily makes conversation and is considered a "good egg," your public relations or dealings with people are probably excellent. But suppose your personality marks you as an introvert who tends to be shy, to withdraw from the crowd, to shun conversation and thereby appear unfriendly? We must agree that your public relations are indeed bad. You may not mean to make a poor impression, but the fact is you do. Unfortunately, we seldom see ourselves through the eyes of the other fellow and we therefore fail to consider what impression our own personal public relations may make on others.

YOUR SCHOOL'S PUBLIC RELATIONS POLICY

Most schools are as popular with young people as a visit to the dentist. You may even have thought that your school purposely went out of its way to make things tough for its students and that it didn't care a fig what the parents thought of its teaching methods. But such is not always true!

Every school is anxious to gain the good will of its students, their parents and the community. The principal and teachers of a tax-supported school know that unless the taxpayers and parents are satisfied with the job they are doing, they may receive no further salary increases and could possibly lose their positions. Most teachers recognize the importance of establishing good relations with the parents of their students. It is for this reason that they freely assist with extracurricular activities, attend P.T.A. meetings and other school events to help accomplish that end. The principal tries to foster a good relationship between the school as a whole and the parents and taxpayers by making school facilities available for certain community activities, inviting parents to special school events and sponsoring various P.T.A. programs.

The trustees and faculty of a college are keenly aware of the necessity for maintaining good public relations not only with the entire public but with the alumni as well. To make ends meet most colleges must be sure of keeping a full enrollment and also obtaining generous financial support from their alumni. It used to be thought a successful football team was all that was necessary to attract applicants for admission. Today few high school seniors pick a college because it boasts an unbeaten eleven. They choose a college on the basis of the reputation it has established either in some particular subject field or as a well-rounded educational institution. This reputation is widespread only if the college has a successful public relations program.

The college or university which depends for its existence upon full enrollment and generous endowment from alumni and other friends of the institution, must be certain that the students and alumni feel friendly toward it and also that the public as a whole looks upon the school with favor. It will be from the general public that the major proportion of future classes will be drawn.

YOUR CHURCH IS AWARE OF PUBLIC RELATIONS TOO

Offhand it would seem that of all institutions a church should have no need to worry about public relations. But wait a minute! What if the minister, priest, or rabbi is unpopular or antagonizes the congregation in one way or another? Do members remain loyal or do they perhaps seek to worship elsewhere? Some congregations are friendly to visitors, some are not. Consider the effect a reputation for being unfriendly would have on newcomers to a town who were "church hunting." A church *should* have no public relations problems but a church is simply a group of human beings who have banded together for common worship. As long as human beings are the unpredictable and often cantankerous creatures they are, a church will have to watch how the actions of its pastor and congregation affect its own members and outsiders too. Enlightened church leaders are aware of the importance of good public relations if their faith is to become an influence in the community and many have undertaken modest public relations programs.

SOCIAL ORGANIZATIONS HAVE PUBLIC RELATIONS PROBLEMS

Again, in the case of a purely social club or organization we might wonder why its members should be concerned with maintaining good public relations. Most clubs exist for the convenience and pleasure of the membership—not the public. Why, then, worry about what Mr. John Q. Public thinks of the club? The answer is simple: no organization can hope to keep its membership or attract new members unless it is well thought of in the community. People join organizations because they are seeking companionship, recreation, or an outlet for their energies. An organization or club with a bad reputation would either attract the wrong people or quickly fold up.

Some years ago at an Eastern college, the fraternity men behaved so badly during a house-party week end that the college canceled future house-party events. The fraternities had created a tough public relations problem both for themselves and for their college. As a result of the unfavorable stories that appeared in the nation's press, the college stood to lose new students, and the fraternities new members. Fortunately the students measured up to their responsibilities. They drew up a code of behavior to be enforced by an interfraternity council and after impressing the college authorities with their intent to behave in the future, the social events were restored. Here was a case of not only regaining a privilege but of re-establishing good relationships between the fraternity and the college as well as restoring the college's reputation with the public.

MOST OF ALL GOVERNMENT REQUIRES GOOD PUBLIC RELATIONS

A politician is the first to recognize the importance of good public relations, particularly if the good will of the voter is essential to continue him in office. Obviously the mayor or the town supervisor and his staff will try to create the best possible impression on the electorate. Few politicians really enjoy kissing babies, laying cornerstones, addressing meetings, smiling at weddings, crying at funerals, making the first donation to the community chest, listening to all kinds of gripes and trying to appease both political parties at the same time. They are smart enough, however, to know that if they would stay in public office they must be seen and known by the public and be all things to all people.

GOOD PUBLIC RELATIONS BRING PROFITS TO BUSINESS

Did you ever notice two drug stores, shoe stores, or grocery stores located on opposite sides of the street? Probably they sell identical merchandise, the service is similar, their prices are equal, yet one enjoys more business than the other. Why?

Since there is no difference in their merchandising policies, there must be something that makes the public show a preference for one. What makes that difference is undoubtedly the public relations policy adopted by the more successful store. This makes people want to patronize it because its owner has carefully cultivated a warm, friendly relationship between its personnel and the public it serves.

TO SUM UP

From the above examples you can see that public relations is a matter of concern to practically everyone in your community. Public relations is something like the atmosphere that surrounds us. When the weather is fair and clear, we scarcely notice it. But when it is foggy, rainy, muggy, or snowy, we are very much aware of our discomfort and annoyance.

However, public relations is much more than the familiar examples described above. Public relations is a profession, a business of its own, a new way of life for industry, government, and a host of other organizations. As we shall see in succeeding chapters, it offers many exciting and rewarding careers to those men and women who grasp its significance, believe in its value, and are eager to bring its benefits to others.

CHAPTER

2

How Public Relations Developed

If you wished to trace the history of public relations from its very beginning, no doubt you would see great significance in the crude pictures found on the walls of caves. You might also attach considerable importance to the *Acta Diurna,* a Roman "daily" which was started during the time of Julius Caesar and published for four centuries. Doubtless you would consider that the campaign which successfully sold the idea of freeing the Holy Land from the infidels and resulted in the colorful Crusades of the Middle Ages, was a tremendous public relations achievement. You should give proper credit to the popularity of the coffee house in England and the salon in France for helping formulate contemporary public opinions. Thomas Jefferson's use of the words "public relations" in his seventh address to the United States Congress in 1807 might contain great historical value.

We suspect, however, that right now you have little interest in the history of the profession. Instead you want to know how you fit into the picture and we therefore refer those readers who may be curious about the historical development of public relations to the list of suggested readings given in Appendix A.

The modern concept of public relations is not only new but still evolving. We cannot properly understand or appreciate the profession unless we very briefly consider the unusual developments of the last half century which completely transformed the old selfish ideas of publicity into the broad and unselfish concept of *benefit to the public* under the newly accepted term of public relations.

Modern public relations has come a long way from the practice of unprincipled publicity pushers like P. T. Barnum whose only concern was to obtain favorable press mentions. The spark that touched off the explosion may have been struck in 1882 when Vanderbilt made his famous "public be damned" remark. Or perhaps it would have happened anyway, for Vanderbilt's callous statement was typical of the attitude of big business and government at that time toward the public.

By the turn of the century industrial expansion, decreasing opportunities on the farm, waves of immigration, and the stubborn individualism and growing power of the capitalist, had made many thinking people realize that the country was undergoing many fundamental social, economic and technological changes. At the same time there was a growing desire for change, change for the better. This was spurred on by the activity of the *muckrakers*—a word coined by President Theodore Roosevelt—who set out to expose the hidden evils of government and business. The muckrakers included such writers as Ida Tarbell who exposed the ruthless practices of the early Standard Oil Company, Lincoln Steffens whose articles pointed up the corruption in city and state governments, Upton Sinclair whose novel, *The Jungle*, revealed the horrors and evils of the meat-packing industry, Ray Stannard Baker whose investigations showed that the railroads got everything they wanted by corrupting politicians and legislatures, and David Graham Phillips, author of *The Treason of the Senate.*

People saw for the first time that what business did and stood for was of concern to *everybody*, not merely a handful of stockholders or financial manipulators. Indeed, President Theodore Roosevelt's administration reflected this new awareness of the public interest with its famous "trustbusting" activities.

During World War I the Committee on Public Information was established under the leadership of George Creel. This was the first time that a planned public relations program was undertaken by the government and its success did much to convince business and industrial leaders that public relations is important to any business undertaking.

Soon more and more leaders in industry and government were realizing that the old concept of publicity was not enough in itself but that intelligent and well planned public relations programs were necessary to mold favorable opinion. Public relations was gradually coming of age, making a complete break from publicity and press agentry.

During the depression of the 1930's when business was under attack from all sides, it was essential that favorable public opinion toward capitalism and the free enterprise system be established if business hoped to escape the threat of socialism. The able men who undertook the task helped develop and perfect many of the techniques which now are common, everyday public relations tools.

With the advent of World War II business and government were well prepared for their respective tasks of informing the public and molding opinion. The government's chief job was to sell *war* to the citizen, the taxpayer, the prospective soldier and his family. Industry's task was twofold: it had to lure to the bench and office millions of new workers, including a high percentage of women, and it had to keep alive its name and good will even though its production was entirely diverted to the military.

Today public relations is a lusty and growing profession. Most corporations are public relations conscious and have one or more full-time employees who devote all their energy to these activities. Innumerable colleges and universities have recognized and honored the profession by establishing public relations courses. In New York City alone, there are almost five hundred public relations counselors listed in the phone directory. It would be difficult to find a field of human endeavor which has not recognized the importance of public relations to its success and put into practice at least some of the principles of this, America's newest and fastest growing profession.

IVY L. LEE

No history of public relations would be complete without mentioning the pioneer of public relations—Ivy L. Lee.

In 1906 the Anthracite Mine Owners were in the throes of a strike and hired the publicity firm of Parker and Lee to serve as press representatives. The outcome of the strike is of little consequence today but the event was worth noting because it gave the junior partner of the firm, Ivy Lee, a job that brought him national recognition. Beginning his career in 1903 as a publicist for the Citizens Union of New York, Lee subsequently worked for the Anthracite Mine Owners, the Pennsylvania Railroad, John D. Rockefeller and a banking firm, before he opened his own New York office on the eve of World War I as a public relations consultant.

Following the war Thomas J. Ross, a man with considerable newspaper experience, joined the firm and assumed many of the managerial duties. In 1933 the firm's name was changed to "Ivy Lee and T. J. Ross." Although Lee died the following year, the firm still bears the name of the man who is generally acknowledged to have been the first public relations counsel.

Lee will probably always be famous for changing the public conception of John D. Rockefeller from that of a ruthless and cruel monopolist to a lovable elderly gentleman who gave dimes to children, played golf, and lived a quiet retiring life. This was achieved by feeding the public countless stories of Rockefeller's charitable and appealing human activities—all designed to change the public's opinion of multi-millionaires.

Ivy Lee believed in keeping the public informed but at the same time humanizing the corporation and the corporation executive. He practiced his public relations on the general public with emphasis on customers, employees, neighbors and friends of the company.

EDWARD L. BERNAYS

Mention should be made of another true pioneer in the field of public relations, Edward L. Bernays, who shares top honors with Ivy Lee. Acknowledged as a founder and leader of the profession, he helped it achieve professional status and recognition at a time when public relations was considered little better than old-fashioned press agentry. It was Mr. Bernays who not only placed public relations in its proper prospective but showed the importance of including public relations in the policy-making operations of every corporation.

A graduate of Cornell University, he first wrote for newspapers before embarking on his career as a publicist. His career has been devoted to counseling on public relations to a host of government agencies, major industrial corporations, trade associations and other groups, in addition to lecturing on public relations, writing several authoritative books on the subject, and serving in a voluntary consulting capacity to various patriotic and charitable organizations.

CHAPTER

3

Communicating with the Public

PUBLIC RELATIONS is not a panacea to solve all problems but in certain given situations it can do an effective job of restoring or creating good will and understanding. Since it acts as a buffer between (1) *a company, organization or group of people,* and (2) *another group of people or the public,* the success of any public relations program depends upon how effectively the first group can communicate (or get its message across) to the second. Methods of communicating, therefore, are basic considerations for the planning of every public relations program. Within the limitations of a single chapter we shall endeavor to discuss briefly the several methods that are available to the public relations director.

HOW SHALL WE REACH THE PUBLIC?

The president of a prominent bus company located in the South called his public relations director to his office.

"George," he said as the portly public relations man eased himself into a red leather chair, "traffic's falling off this month, probably as a result of those two accidents on the West Coast. How are we going to convince the public that traveling by bus is safe?"

"With our swell safety record that shouldn't be hard," the public relations man replied. He leaned back in the chair, closed his eyes and thought for a moment.

"First, we'll get some stories in the papers. That's easy, and I'll have Dick do a few magazine articles which shouldn't be hard to place in Rotary, Kiwanis, Chamber of Commerce and similar magazines. We've got some good film just shot in the garage showing our new maintenance program. I know a couple of television stations that will be glad to use it. We might get it shown before some clubs and other groups too."

He rose, paced the floor a moment, then faced the president.

"Say, there's that new chap we hired from the radio station to cover both radio and television. With the good story we have to tell, plus his know-how, we should have no trouble getting our share of mentions on the air."

"Sounds O.K. to me," the president agreed. "Now let's see, —newspapers, radio, television. That's fine, but how about word of mouth and books too? They are important ways to get our message across, aren't they?"

"Of course, but give me time to think this out," the public relations director insisted. He studied his shoes for a few moments, then continued: "Word of mouth, you know, can be a ticklish proposition. We want to be sure that we get the *right* story started. Now, if we should write our twenty-five thousand shareholders and our fifteen hundred employees and get them to tell their friends about our safety record and what swell service we're offering on the streamliner, we should generate a lot of good conversation in this part of Dixie. Naturally we will schedule several press conferences in the larger cities we serve." He shoved his hands in his coat pockets, fished around a bit, took out a pack of cigarettes, and then lit one.

"As for books,—they take too long to come out to do us any

good right now. The way I understand the problem, we want to re-establish the public's confidence just as quickly as possible." The president nodded in agreement.

"For your information," the public relations man explained, "we are in contact with a couple of graduate students at the university who are writing a study of transportation in the South. We're watching this field closely."

And so a public relations program, designed to gain the understanding and confidence of the public, is born and the channels of communication selected. Now for a look at each of these methods of communicating ideas: the press, magazines, radio, movies, television, direct mail, word of mouth, conferences and books.

NEWSPAPERS

There are more than ten thousand newspapers published in the United States, an average of over one and a quarter per family being printed daily. Practically every adult reads a newspaper at least once a week; most of us who are interested in keeping up with what is going on in the world about us read a paper every day.

Newspapers are an ideal means of placing information before large groups of people. It is true that generally a news item is read but once and the paper then discarded. Nevertheless the story enjoys a wide circulation; often it may make a fairly lasting impression on the reader and may be clipped for future use.

How does a newspaper gather its news? It cannot afford to have reporters scattered throughout the country, or the world, for that matter. Years ago several newspapers attempted to solve this part of their news-gathering problem by banding together and forming the Associated Press. This organization has representatives or facilities for gathering news from the four corners of the globe and, since its formation, has been joined by two competitors, the United Press and the International News Service. By belonging to one or more of these news-gathering services, a paper is assured of good coverage on significant news events occurring outside its own city. Staff reporters are employed for covering its local area.

Few people realize how much news is actually "planted." Many, many stories in your daily paper are written by professional writers employed by business concerns, trade organizations and the government. Practically all the major news items appearing in the financial, business, and real estate sections are so inspired. Special news stories about spectacular inventions, discoveries, business milestones, or product development are similarly planted. Almost all news about government activities comes from press releases or press conferences conducted for the benefit of the press by the public relations officer of the government agency. Social items such as news stories of engagements, weddings, coming-out parties, teas, dinner parties attended by prominent citizens, etc., are often written and sent to the paper by the bride's parents or the hostess of the party.

There is no intention here to minimize the work of the newspaper reporter but to suggest how news is gathered and why some stories are necessarily planted. Imagine yourself the publisher and star reporter for a newspaper in a typical small city. You must depend on the wire services for your out-of-town, national, and international news. But how do you drum up local news? You never could afford to hire enough reporters to call daily on all the business concerns in your city, merely on the chance that they might have a hot news story for you. At best you can cover city hall, the police station, and an occasional four-alarm fire. But for the real estate, business, and financial news you must rely on the publicity releases sent to you by the various public relations departments of your local industry. Fortunately, the writer of the press release is usually more anxious for you to print his story than you may be to receive it. Thus you are practically assured of a steady flow of incoming news that helps fill your paper as well as insure good news coverage of business activity in your town. It is a sensible and legitimate way of gathering news.

MAGAZINES

One glance at any newsstand where a fairly complete stock of periodicals is carried will convince you that there are magazines galore, enough to suit every conceivable taste and interest. Look at the vast numbers of people reached by each single issue of the following magazines:

Life	26,450,000
Look	18,050,000
Saturday Evening Post	14,050,000
Ladies Home Journal	11,500,000

It has been estimated that a single issue of the *Reader's Digest* reaches 13,000,000 people, 5,000,000 of whom live in foreign countries.

Magazines generally are kept longer than newspapers. There is a tendency on the part of the public to consider magazine articles as fairly authoritative, perhaps because the format of the average magazine is impressive and the editorial board is given more credit than it sometimes deserves for verifying the accuracy of the information presented. If the old saying that one picture is worth a thousand words is still true, consider the value to a company of a picture showing its product or service which is accepted by *Life* magazine, for instance!

The magazines you see displayed at your newsdealer comprise only a portion of all periodicals printed in this country. In addition to the general magazines, such as *The Saturday Evening Post* and *Collier's,* news magazines like *Time, Newsweek, Pathfinder,* and picture magazines like *Life, Look, See,* you will find a wide selection of women's magazines, humor, digest, love, comic, sport, adventure, detective, hobby, etc. Obviously most of these are not suitable vehicles for carrying your article that aims to create better understanding of your organization or news of some development which you believe will be of interest to the public.

But there are other important magazines which, although they may not enjoy distribution on all newsstands, nevertheless boast substantial circulations among influential men and women who are leaders or policy molders in their profession or business. The more important of these are: Business Reviews; i.e., *Harvard Business Review;* Business and Financial Magazines; i.e., *Business Week, Fortune, Forbes, Barrons;* Trade Magazines; i.e., *Bus Transportation, Oil and Gas Journal;* Professional Journals; i.e., *Michigan Law Review, Journal of the American Statistical Association.*

You can readily see that there is a wide variety of readers available to the public relations director, but in order to reach effectively each interest group, he may have to write the story several times, slanting each version for one particular magazine. Better yet, he may succeed in interesting the editor in his "story," whereupon a magazine staff writer will be assigned to sit down with him, get the facts, and then go back to his office to turn out the finished article.

RADIO

Many radio stations broadcast twenty-four hours a day and offer innumerable opportunities for communicating with their vast audience through regular programs, spot announcements, newscasts, and special mentions worked into a script.

Surveys show that radio, despite the growing acceptance of television, is not decreasing in popularity. In many homes radio is considered such a necessity that two or three are required to satisfy the needs of various members of the family. Radio has the advantage of not requiring our undivided attention, as is the case of reading or watching television. A person can be working or playing, yet still listen to the radio and be mentally receptive to the spoken word. A recent survey showed that about half the families in the United States consider radio a necessity. Practically no one with television is without radio and a fifth of the population owns three to seven radios. In 1955 there were about 3,200 radio stations compared with 600 television stations.

MOVIES

Hollywood Produced—Occasionally a company is fortunate enough to have its name and product shown in a newsreel or feature picture. Thus, a radically new automobile, the opening of a luxurious resort hotel, the inaugural flight of a new airplane service, the development of a wonder drug or chemical, will often bring out the newsreel men.

Now and then the shooting of regular feature films provides opportunities for a business enterprise to get its name into the movies. As the scenario unfolds, the actors may travel and some form of transportation may benefit by having its name appear. The stars may visit famous places, (the observatory of the Empire State Building, for instance), use well-known or "brand" name products (such as ride in a Cadillac), and directly or indirectly call attention to the products or services of many companies. Some concerns that sell nationally have on their public relations staff one or more members who are familiar with the techniques of producing movies as well as with important men and women in the film world.

Sponsored Films—Each year more and more films are being sponsored (paid for) by business and industry to interest people in the organization, to sell the product, to inform the employees and shareholders, to influence public opinion, or to educate the public. Such films are distributed nationally and usually are available for projection before service clubs, women's clubs, professional societies, schools, trade organizations, churches, civic groups and other meetings, as well as for use on television. You will find that many sponsored films purposely run either 14 or 28 minutes to conform to the requirements of a tight television time schedule and thus hope to interest the program manager of one or more television stations. Unless a public relations film is entertaining and the company name is rarely mentioned, movie theater managers will not be interested.

Typical of such films are the following two releases which, although educational, are part of a definite public relations program:

"Good Place to Work," sponsored by the National Association of Manufacturers. The film shows current and past achievements of industry in improving factory working conditions. It was designed to correct the wrong impression many high school students have about factory work.

"Black Diamonds, the Story of Anthracite," sponsored by the Anthracite Information Bureau. This film tells the story of anthracite but emphasizes the future of anthracite as a heating fuel. It is an excellent example of how a sick industry is trying to recapture public favor through the medium of film.

Sponsored films are expensive to produce, are generally unacceptable to local theaters, and appeal to a limited audience. However, they are highly useful to a public relations director who wants to get a message across to a very specialized group which he knows will come see the film.

Consider the case of a food processor accused by the government of making excessive profits. Its public relations director might decide to tell the management's side of the story to its owners, employees, distributors, and such segments of the public as it can reach. A film explaining the company's annual report would be a perfect vehicle for a story of this kind because it could show why profits are necessary, what was done with them, and—more important still—how the company benefited the public. The film could be shown at shareholders' meetings and to every employee, as well as be made available for distributor conferences and interested outside groups or organizations.

A good film can do a powerful public relations job, but to achieve its purpose ways and means must be devised of showing it to the very people whom it is intended to influence. This is not always done and many a good public relations film has sat on the shelves for want of proper distribution.

TELEVISION

The impact of television upon the thinking and behavior of the American adult is not as perceptible as its effect on children. Grade school teachers deplore the indiscriminate use of television in the home by younger children because of its effect upon their thinking and behavior. But what a marvelous vehicle we have in television to influence public opinion by visually bringing a story or message right into the home! What could be better than to appeal to the eye and the ear simultaneously?

Television is developing by leaps and bounds. Like radio, its needs for program material are almost insatiable and it presents unlimited opportunities to the public relations director who wants to use this excellent medium to communicate with the public.

DIRECT MAIL

Letters are usually written to convey news to the addressee. Social letters may bear tidings of love, sorrow, personal achievement, family doings, or a host of other matters. Business letters may inform, solicit business, close a sale, request payment, answer a complaint, explain a mistake, demand payment of a bill, or perform a variety of duties. Every letter is an expression of the writer's personality and his or her company is judged by the letter he writes. Good letter writing is therefore good public relations.

Letter writing is one of the oldest methods of communicating with others. With our swift and efficient postal system, it is the surest way of reaching people at a very modest cost per letter. For the public relations program that must get its message to a comparatively small or selective group of customers, distributors, agents, salesman, public officials, or others, direct mail is an ideal media. But to reach large segments of the public by direct mail is often impractical because of the difficulty and the high cost of compiling mailing lists.

Many large service companies have customer relations departments which, although they may report to the sales department, are actually performing a daily public relations function. Usually their chief duty is to answer letters of complaint.

In the case of important policy-making correspondence prepared for or by executives, such letters are generally double checked with the public relations department lest something be said that is not consistent with the company's over-all public relations policy.

MOUTH TO MOUTH

The very oldest form of communication is the person-to-person or word-of-mouth method, but as a tool for the public relations man it has very limited value.

In the small village, years ago, Ye Towne Crier made his rounds announcing the time and important news happenings. It was no problem then to spread news or to communicate with the townspeople. Today, our urban areas are so densely populated that many people living in an apartment house don't know their next-door neighbor. Those who live on isolated farms and ranches get little or no information from neighbors unless they take the trouble to listen in on their party line—and many do!

It is quite apparent that no attempt to communicate with a large segment of the public by relying on people to pass the message from mouth to mouth is going to succeed. When a message can be sent to carefully selected groups of people who have an interest in a particular matter and they are asked to tell their friends, as in the case of the employees and shareholders of the bus company, some good results may be achieved.

It is true that gossip, or jokes told at the expense of a politician or a prominent person, find their way around the country quickly. Also, when a smear campaign is resorted to, the ugly rumors circulate readily. People are always eager to tell their friends something that is sensational, funny, or mean. For such people factual information lacks zest for teller and listener alike.

CONFERENCE

When a company has news which it considers unusually important, it may decide to invite reporters to attend a special press conference at which the president, the vice-president of public relations, or another appropriate official will tell his story and answer questions. A press conference may also be arranged when an important executive is visiting a city distant from the company's home office and it seems desirable to expose him to the questions of local reporters.

A conference or special meeting might be held by a drug manufacturer, for instance, who wanted to show a new development in medical research to certain doctors and reporters for medical journals. This is an ideal means of spreading news about the new product and giving those people most interested a firsthand opportunity to examine it and ask questions.

Note that the gatherings referred to above are primarily for the purpose of disseminating news. Another type of conference, in this case a dignified name for a cocktail party, is often held to entertain key or important individuals. This "conference" is an ideal opportunity to create good will and to explain a particular policy, action, or position of the company which may need the support of a selected group. Such a conference would provide an excellent means for a trade association to explain to the town fathers its members' problems and need for tax relief.

Open house, tours, special meetings, dinners, picnics, etc., for owners, customers, or the public, give a company an excellent opportunity to entertain and influence large groups of people at one time. This type of conference is not held to give out a news story but rather to create a cordial atmosphere and lead to a better understanding of the company's problems.

BOOKS

Books also offer another method of communicating ideas. However, they have three serious drawbacks which place them at the bottom of our list. First, there is necessarily too great a time lag between the writing and the publication of the average book. Many public relations programs cannot afford to wait three to twelve months to present their message. Second, unfortunately, most Americans are not book readers although our country has one of the highest rates of literacy in the world. Too few people have the time or desire to read anything other than newspapers, magazines and—to judge from the newsstands and bookstores—the lurid variety of pocket books. Third, the price of the average book (unless it is an inexpensive pocket edition) may keep it from the very people to whom its message is directed.

On the other hand, a book enables a company, organization, or government agency to present a complete story to the reader and, through pictures and text, leave a lasting and convincing impression. Corporations hire professional writers to tell their history and purpose in such an interesting and readable manner that such books are often sold through regular trade channels. Biographies of presidents, leaders of industry and government, scientists, professional men and women, and a host of other prominent people are perfect vehicles for influencing public opinion in one way or another. As noted in the previous chapter, the muckrakers of the 1890's used books to carry their message to the public.

Books may play an important role as part of a long range public relations program but by their nature they are not capable of carrying a message swiftly to a large audience.

IN CONCLUSION

The ability to communicate with others is as essential to public relations as a well maintained right of way is to a railroad. Therefore, the success of every public relations program depends not only on a carefully conceived and well thought out plan that is designed to produce the desired

CHAPTER

4

Publicity and Promotion

JEAN MARTIN, an unknown but aspiring movie starlet, met an enterprising press agent who promised to introduce her to a leading movie producer and make her a star overnight if she would let him act as her manager. Miss Martin readily agreed and the following Tuesday morning the starlet and her new manager arrived by day coach at New York's Grand Central Station. They were met at the gate by a little man who carried a shiny black satchel.

"Meet my friend, Sam," the press agent said to the would-be actress. "He'll check our bags and then go with us to Mr. Luckor's office."

As soon as the shabby baggage was hidden in a locker, the trio proceeded through the terminal and out to 42nd Street.

"It's only a couple of blocks," the agent explained, "so we'll hoof it."

As they walked toward Madison Avenue, Sam dropped behind and stealthily reached into the black bag. Suddenly he scattered several handfuls of pennies, then as he continued behind his employer, he dribbled a steady stream of coins to lure further the greedy and growing crowd that followed.

Immediately upon reaching Mr. Luckor's building, the press agent led Miss Martin inside while Sam stayed on the sidewalk to throw the remaining pennies at the excited crowd. His supply was soon exhausted, whereupon he disappeared into the subway.

Upstairs on the fifteenth floor the press agent burst breathlessly into the movie producer's office.

"Morning, Mr. Luckor. Just arrived on the Century with Miss Martin. Boy, what a reception she got! You better take my advice and sign her up pronto for the lead in your new picture. Come, look at the crowd that followed us from the station!"

Mr. Luckor reluctantly struggled out of his chair, waddled to the window, and peered below. The cigar dropped from his mouth as he stared incredulously at the mob that filled the street.

"Have Miss Martin come right in," he barked, "I simply must have her for my picture!"

Miss Martin signed the contract that morning.

This story, which is said actually to have happened, is an example of the type of special build-up or stunt planned by a press agent which gave publicity a dubious reputation. You will recall that before the development of modern public relations, a lot of publicity was conjured up by rather irresponsible promoters, press agents, and other ballyhoo artists who had no code of ethics to guide them. They believed that in order to call attention to someone or something it was permissible and often necessary to resort to hoaxes, chicanery, and humbug. Although they were often successful in accomplishing their immediate purpose, their methods won them no public acclaim.

This kind of press agent still exists. He transforms the mediocre actress into a Hollywood star, makes a person or place famous, and plants pictures of movie stars, bathing beauties and other lovelies in your evening paper. This is press agentry, pure and simple. Under no circumstances should it be confused with public relations.

WHAT IS PUBLICITY?

Public relations, you remember, is dealing successfully with people, the emphasis being placed on an activity that is beneficial to the public or a special group. Public relations is an over-all plan or purpose—the guide book but not the means of achieving the end result. To accomplish an agreed-upon program, public relations men use three principal tools: *publicity, promotion,* and *advertising.* (We will discuss advertising in the next chapter).

Publicity is news. It informs people about the policy laid down by the public relations program. It is the means of getting the public relations idea accepted and known. Publicity's principal function is to disseminate news about the organization or company it serves in order to build good will.

Public relations is a plan for living well and telling others about it. Publicity is the means of telling others about the living. True publicity is "information with a news value designed to advance the interests of a place, person, cause or institution, usually appearing in public print." * Publicity cannot be purchased and therein greatly differs from advertising.

Publicity is "information with news value" but do not expect that the information will necessarily be educational or edifying to the reader. To have news value a publicity item can also be sensational, morbid, or ludicrous. It can work for you as well as against you. In fact, a public relations department sometimes must go "into reverse" when something of an unpleasant nature suddenly becomes "information with news value." Thus, if a department store suffers

* Webster's New International Dictionary.

a freak fire and several customers lose their lives, the public relations department will do everything possible to cooperate with the press to see that the reporters have the facts surrounding the catastrophe, that all their questions are answered factually and honestly, and that they are provided, if possible, with facilities for writing and sending their stories. No one can suppress such front page news but a good public relations man can get sympathetic treatment from the press.

Thus, a reporter who suspected that the store was holding back information and was being uncooperative might play up a false rumor that made the management appear negligent. If the same reporter felt that he had the facts and that the company officials were giving him all the help he needed to prepare his story, he might give emphasis to the angle that the store was not at fault. This would be valuable publicity for a business whose management is anxious to restore public confidence.

Although use of the word *publicity* is rapidly losing ground to *public relations*, there are still many reputable institutions that have publicity bureaus and directors of publicity. Don't be prejudiced against a publicity department because of the unsavory reputation the word *publicity* has gained in the past. A real publicity bureau is devoted to putting out genuine news stories or telling others about the organization. A publicity bureau or department usually exists when there is no public relations department within which this function would normally be centered. Boston University, for example, has a publicity department for the purpose of keeping the public informed about the university.

PROMOTION

Promotion is a popular word in the lexicon of both the public relations director and the sales manager. A promotion is any special activity that strives to gain attention. It need have no other purpose and, unlike public relations, it need not of itself benefit the public or a selected group. Nor is it necessarily "information with a news value." It is simply an attention-getter and as such is a useful tool for the public relations director. Bear in mind, however, that it never becomes a substitute for publicity and advertising, the two principal means of disseminating information. A promotion need not impart information or news. Rather, it is often used first to catch the eye or ear so that the individual will be attentive to the publicity or the advertising message that follows.

At this point we must differentiate between publicity and promotion. The word *promotion* sometimes serves as an all-inclusive term when used to describe the conduct of a public relations plan. A public relations director may decide that the success of his plan cannot be achieved by limiting his activity just to publicity and advertising. He may consider it necessary to attract public attention through stunts such as contests, pageants, lucky prizes, free rides, a joint effort with another company, or a host of other gimmicks. All of this effort, when coupled with publicity and perhaps advertising too, is frequently referred to as a promotion or promotional campaign. It is the means of successfully accomplishing a public relations plan.

A word of caution! Do not confuse the use of the word *promotion* in a public relations program with promotions staged by the old style publicity man or press agent who was always "promoting" something and whose stock in trade was the sensational or unusual. Nor are we referring here to the modern sales promotion campaign that precedes the introduction of a new product or an intensive selling effort. Deceptive or spectacular promotions have no place in today's genuine public relations program. However, "gimmicks" or novel stunts may be used effectively if they are not fraudulent.

Examples of public relations promotions that do not use publicity or advertising:

As part of its day-to-day public relations responsibility for keeping the name of the company before the public (remembering the emphasis on benefit to the public), an airline made available an airplane for an important scientific expedition. As a result, the company's name was featured in the headlines and the public should have been favorably impressed. Excellent publicity was the *result* of this promotion.

R. H. Macy & Company stages an annual Thanksgiving Day parade in New York which features comic performers, elaborate floats, mammoth balloons shaped like animals, and elaborate displays. No advertising is directed at the thousands of people who watch the event from the sidewalks or their television sets. The parade is not an advertisement of Macy's merchandise. It is not publicity since it imparts no information. It is, however, a promotion which as part of the over-all public relations program aims to create good will and keep the public ever aware of the store. (Incidentally it always generates lots of valuable publicity!)

A gift of four new sewing machines to the New York Herald Tribune Fresh Air Fund reaped some good publicity for the Necchi Sewing Machine Sales Corporation. A picture of a camper using one of the machines (its trade name quite visible) appeared in the *Herald Tribune* over a caption telling about the sewing courses made possible for the campers.

THE JOB TO BE DONE

Perhaps you can better understand the respective roles publicity and promotion play in a public relations program after you look in on Ellen Banks, public relations director for a large metropolitan hotel. As we first eavesdropped, the attractive brunette was sitting at her desk, reviewing the hotel's public relations program with Dick, her tall, lanky assistant.

"Your staff seems to be doing a swell over-all publicity job," Miss Banks commented as she thumbed through the thick scrapbook containing all the "clips" of newspaper and magazine stories that mentioned the hotel. "Tell them to keep up the good work; you know how forgetful the public can be. Now, let's see, how about briefing me on our labor problem?"

Dick opened the folder that lay on his lap and handed a file folder across the desk to his boss.

"Here are the details for your approval. I met with Page, our new personnel manager, and from what he tells me, the situation is worse than we thought. It's almost impossible to find people who will work for us since the hotel acquired such a reputation for bad working conditions, poor pay, and long hours. Of course, Page cleaned up the mess but we must get the facts across to labor if we hope to build up a decent staff."

Miss Banks drummed her fingers on the red desk blotter.

"This is very serious. When such a reputation gets around it takes a lot of persuasion to change public opinion and particularly that of a suspicious applicant."

"Right," Dick agreed, "but I think we've mapped out a good program. First, we'll give the papers a steady stream of news and pictures showing our improved facilities, our new employee lounge, and the recreation hall. The press will also receive a lot of good dope on our new pay scales, hours of work, paid holidays, and other employee benefits. Then, we plan to call on the manager of every employment agency and invite him, his interviewers and their wives, to a special dinner and tour of the hotel next Friday night. Unless I miss my bet, they'll all be here for the free meal, and. . . ."

"Wait a minute!" Miss Banks interrupted as she pushed her chair back. "How about inviting the press too? This should make a darn good story."

"But, of course, why didn't I think of it myself?" her assistant moaned. "By the way, we're getting attractive souvenirs for every guest: compacts for the ladies, lighters for the men—each decorated with the hotel's emblem."

"So far so good, but haven't you overlooked the possibility of doing some advertising?" the public relations director asked.

"No, I'm working with the advertising agency along the general idea of telling the public what a great place this is to stay, eat, entertain, and work. Another series of ads will feature our employee benefits. Why, even the boiler room will sound like the best place in town to work! You'll see the final agency copy in a day or so."

"All right. Now, one special promotion we must plan immediately is for the new Baroque Room which opens next month. The orchestra and floor show will require fancy prices, so we should make our pitch to the social set and the upper income group. Do you think you could get the mayor and his wife for the opening? She should cut the ribbon to open the room officially."

"I'll try but if they can't make it, how about Mrs. Randolph Fleming? She's president of the Federated Women's Club, and does she love publicity for herself!"

They both laughed as they mentally pictured the bejeweled dowager beaming at the photographers. Mrs. Fleming would never guess she was a pawn of the hotel's public relations department.

"She'd be excellent, but let's not forget the younger set too. See if the Junior League would like to sponsor a dance for their pet charity. The management has agreed to donate exclusive use of the room plus music, floor show, and waiter service on a Monday night when the room will normally be closed. The gals can sell their own tickets and it will help introduce us to that crowd."

Miss Banks walked to the window, raised the venetian blinds and studied the city's skyline for a moment. Her back still to Dick, she said:

"I heard that the Golwin Studios are going to shoot a movie about life and love in a hotel. Think of the publicity we could get if it were shot here and our name appeared even once or twice! Go over and see if you can sell them on the advantages of taking several scenes downstairs. Show them some pictures of the lobby with its double-tiered balcony, the kitchens, dining rooms, etc. They might fall for the idea. Then. . . ."

And so the plans were discussed and agreed upon.

Now if you will review this conversation you will see that our alert director and her capable assistant discussed four different public relations activities:

1. *The Day-to-Day Job.* There is a daily routine publicity job to be done in every public relations office. The object, of course, is to keep the name of the organization before the public. This includes issuing press releases whenever there is a newsworthy story, answering telephone calls, entertaining visitors, calling on prospects who might print, broadcast, or televise information of one kind or another, and being constantly on tap to handle the unexpected or an emergency. The "clip book" referred to on page 35 is a record of all news items and pictures that have appeared in print. It provides evidence of the department's accomplishments and is particularly valuable when budget time rolls around.

2. *An Important Management Problem.* When a bad labor relations problem arose, the personnel manager sought the help and advice of the public relations director. The unique

plan discussed for solving this crisis was an undertaking for which the public relations department was well suited.

3. *Joint Promotion with the Sales Department.* The public relations department is frequently called upon to assist the sales department in the promotion of a new service or product. In this case the public relations staff had the necessary experience as well as the entree to prominent people.

4. *Seeking Special Outlets for Promotions.* There are many ways of keeping one's name before the public that do not result from issuing news releases. By offering one's facilities or services to other companies or organizations that may be able to use them advantageously, good publicity may result.

Filming of the movie in the hotel would not only bring famous stars into the establishment and attract a host of movie fans, but would get the name and actual pictures of the hotel into the film itself. Unlimited publicity on a national scale could result from such a promotion.

In a somewhat similar manner an airline offered an unusual facility to the television networks. Because the action of many television dramas and shows takes place in airplanes, American Airlines built a special model of a cabin interior which is made available free of charge to any television station requesting it. This saved the producer the cost of building a set, assured the audience of authentic staging, and gave the airline an opportunity to get its name before the television audience as well as build up good will among the television fraternity.

SUMMARY

Planting publicity in newspapers, magazines, radio programs, etc., is not always easy. This is a highly competitive field and a press release must really have "information with a news value" to qualify it for consideration by the editor.

It is difficult to evaluate the effectiveness of publicity.

There is no way of measuring its impact upon the public, no way of telling if people are impressed or even see or read it. The public relations director may take such comfort and encouragement as he can from a well filled "clip book" but clippings measured in inches are difficult to appraise because of the difference in circulation and value between newspapers and magazines.

Publicity and promotion are two of the most intangible activities ever conceived but when intelligently planned and carried out, they can prove extremely effective in helping achieve a public relations objective—as many, many companies have learned. Were this not so, there would be no public relations department in business and industry. Today there is scarcely a major company without one.

CHAPTER

5

Public Relations and Advertising

As Frank McClaren *carefully piloted his sleek truck-trailer toward Clinton, Iowa, headquarters of his employer, Carstensen Freight Lines, a blue sedan shot past him in the crisp air of an October day.*

Then it happened!

The blue sedan tried to pass the car ahead of Frank—a green convertible—cut in too fast and sideswiped it, sending both cars out of control. The green convertible struck the rough shoulder and its curb-side door flew open, catapulting a woman into the canal that ran alongside the road.

Instantly Frank parked his truck-trailer, plunged into the cold water and rescued the unconscious woman. And, as other truck drivers pulled up, he removed an injured man from the blue sedan and helped free two children caught in the wreckage.

Acts of heroism like this—for which Frank McClaren was named Iowa's "Driver of the Month"—typify America's gentlemen of the highways, our truck drivers.

Their main job, of course, is to keep the freight moving, for everything you eat, wear, and use travels at least part of the way to you by truck.

But they do more than this, these truck drivers.

They set a pattern for safe, courteous driving on our highways. And when there's trouble, they're nearly always the first to lend a helping hand.

This reads more like an article re-condensed from the *Reader's Digest* than an advertisement of the American Trucking Industry which appeared in *The Wall Street Journal.* It represents a recent development in the field of public relations advertising and you can see that it differs greatly from the usual kind of advertising which confronts us daily.

There are three types of advertising, each of which you will readily recognize without any difficulty. They are:

Product advertising that promotes the sale of goods or services. Most advertising sells a product or service.

Institutional advertising which strives to create in the public mind friendship and a feeling of respect for the company or organization that is sponsoring the advertisement. The American Trucking Industry ad is a good example of this type.

Public Relations advertising that performs a service for the public by endeavoring to persuade people to do something that is beneficial to them. You see such advertisements particularly prior to a presidential election when public-spirited companies urge local citizens to get out and vote.

The practice of using advertising to sell ideas as well as products or services is fairly new. Because it is important to the public relations director, let's explore the significance of institutional and public relations advertising a bit further.

INSTITUTIONAL ADVERTISING

During World War II many large companies were forced to divert their production from consumer goods to munitions. General Motors manufactured practically no cars for sale to the public but devoted its entire production to trucks, tanks, airplane engines and parts, etc. During this four-year period the public might well have forgotten the company and its reputation had it not been for the constant advertising program which told about General Motors' wartime activities and the new cars the company was planning to bring again to Americans after victory. Because many other companies were similarly affected, the newspapers carried many advertisements that offered nothing for sale but merely mentioned the company's war effort or plans for peacetime production.

Some Bell Telephone System ads tell us about the "voice with the smile," the heroism of an employee, or a new technological development in telephone communication. There is no urging to make greater use of the phone or to place long distance calls in much of this copy. In fact, some people wonder why the Bell System advertises at all, since the telephone is an everyday and necessary means of communication. But the company wisely reasons that a service industry must constantly cultivate public friendship and understanding for the company and its problems. As a result of such a program, it is hoped that the public will be more sympathetic and tolerant when the company applies for a rate increase or there is an unexpected breakdown of equipment.

PUBLIC RELATIONS ADVERTISING

To most of us the word *advertising* suggests a full or partial page in our newspaper or magazine which is so skillfully written or arranged that it makes us crave the product or service offered. Practically all the advertisements we see are pushing the sale of products or services. They aim to sell something, and if effective, serve as a powerful sales tool. But occasionally we find one that is not giving us a sales pitch. In fact it is disarmingly tame and unselfish. It may give us health advice, remind us to drive safely, exhort us to read the Bible, tell us of the outstanding service performed by certain employees of a company, or even reprint an editorial on a burning issue of the day.

These are *public relations* advertisements because they bring a message from the owners or management which is beneficial to the public and which they believe the public should share. At the same time the advertisements are building up good will because you, the reader, link the name of the company with its altruistic message.

Don't you suppose that the trucking industry ad was placed in *The Wall Street Journal* to cultivate the friendship of the businessman (the shipper) for the trucking industry? The same advertisement placed in the New York *Times* or *The Saturday Evening Post* would probably be aimed at mollifying the pleasure driver who finds the presence of large trucks on the highway annoying. The next time your neighbor is stuck on a hill behind a slow truck, the advertiser hopes he will remember the behavior of Frank McClaren and grin and bear it.

You will note that most of the Metropolitan Life Insurance Company's periodical advertising urges people to take better care of their health and offers good health pointers. As a further public service the company offers to send free booklets of advice. No mention is made in the advertisements about buying insurance and those who request literature are never solicited by a salesman. The name of the company is associated in your mind with sane, healthy living, a good connotation. Such advertising benefits you and the company. For you, better health means longer living and for the insurance company, longevity brings better earnings which ultimately result in lower premiums to the insured.

The Texas and Pacific Railroad conducted an unusual advertising campaign in the early 1950's. This campaign was strictly religious with no mention of the railroad's rates, service, or station locations. The copy, which spoke of faith in God and our country, was prepared by the president and the director of employee-public relations. The ads were read too! Letters poured in from all over the world and three million copies of a pamphlet reproducing the advertisement were distributed.

Another believer in religious advertising as a public service is a successful real estate developer, Leon Ackerman, of Washington, D.C., whose full-page advertisements have appeared since 1952 in leading papers throughout the country. Each advertisement brings a short message from the Bible. "I am an individual trying to spread the Gospel of Love among the greatest number of people," Mr. Ackerman says. "I use the press for this advertising as I think this is the best way to command an audience greater, perhaps, than church or lecture hall attendance." Although he desires to remain anonymous, the newspapers insisted on a personal identification after their switchboards were flooded with calls asking for information about the advertiser. No mention is ever made of his business affiliation. "My sole objective in spending so much of my income in spreading this message," declares Mr. Ackerman, "is because of my love for and appreciation of American democracy and American institutions and of the land from which I have received so many blessings in abundance; and this is my only motive."

The cost of institutional or public relations advertising must be charged to the public relations budget. It is not sales expense and it must be carefully planned and integrated into the over-all public relations program to make sure that the company is getting its money's worth.

WHERE SHALL WE ADVERTISE?

Institutional or public relations advertising need not be limited only to newspapers and periodicals. Radio, television, direct mail, displays and signs are sometime even more effective media for the public relations director to use. But which shall he choose?

Newspapers? Yes, if we want to reach a certain group of people who are subscribers to a particular newspaper. In a small town an advertising message would reach almost every family if placed in the local paper. In a large city it would probably be necessary to advertise in several newspapers to insure good coverage. The subscribers to most papers live within a fairly well-defined area that gives the advertiser a good idea of where his message will go. If there is an urgency in getting our message before the public, a newspaper is well equipped to handle our need for quick service. However, as previously suggested, newspapers are perishable commodities and if the reader did not see our message when he first read through his paper, we have doubtless failed to reach him in that issue.

Magazines? Magazine advertising as part of our public relations program is good for reaching a wider audience than that found among the readers of newspapers. A periodical has the advantage of being retained longer than a newspaper and of being picked up more than once.

Radio or Television? Shall we appeal to the ear and/or the eye, perhaps by spicing our message with entertainment? Television, in particular, lends itself for effective advertising where it is possible to give a visual presentation of our message.

Outstanding examples of *radio institutional* and *public relations* advertising programs are the United States Steel "Theater Guild on the Air" and the Chicago *Tribune* "Theater of the Air." Neither of these sponsors advertise their products (steel and advertising, respectively).

The United States Steel program, in addition to entertaining, brings an informative message each week about the company and the steel industry. The musical portion of the "Theater of the Air" program was preceded by a talk by the late Colonel Robert R. McCormick, editor and publisher of the newspaper. He took this opportunity to present his views on a number of subjects of interest to him, many with a patriotic theme but none carrying any mention of the newspaper.

Direct Mail? Yes, if we have a specific group to be reached, for we know that the first requirement of a direct mail campaign is a good live mailing list. We can consider as prospects the following: employees, shareholders, customers, distributors, competitors, members of a political body or organization; in short, any group for which a membership roster or mailing list is available.

Direct mail is an excellent means of putting across a message to a special group. However, if our public relations man wants to reach large numbers of people, he would probably find it wiser to consider other means of public relations advertising because direct mail is expensive and, unless accurate mailing lists are used, the money appropriated for this purpose may be wasted.

Billboards and Displays? Billboard advertising will reach many people if our boards are located on busy highways or streets. Local industry often rents billboard space to identify the city to visitors, to assist a civic undertaking, to help a charitable drive for funds, or to cooperate in a health campaign. You have seen countless such signs:

WELCOME TO ROLLING SPRING

Home of Excello Mineral Water

DRIVE CAREFULLY—THE LIFE YOU SAVE MAY BE YOUR OWN

A Public Service Reminder of the Acme Gasoline Company

SUPPORT YOUR COMMUNITY CHEST DRIVE

Jones Manufacturing Company

Display or card advertising in trains, street cars, busses and taxis show your message again and again to the same people, probably more often than through any other form of advertising. Such advertisements, when placed in the public interest, usually urge support of a patriotic, charitable, or civic undertaking.

Portable display units that can be set up in donated or rented space at travel shows, open houses, church affairs, educational exhibits, country fairs, etc., provide an opportunity for the public to become better acquainted with the usage of the company's product or service or a new scientific development.

As an aid to the Ground Observer Corps of the United States Air Force, the New York Telephone Company constructed and made available for demonstration a working model that showed how radar operates. This had absolutely nothing to do with telephone service but was extremely useful in explaining the need for volunteers to man the nation's thousands of ground observer posts as aircraft spotters because enemy aircraft could, under certain conditions, avoid detection by radar. Here is an outstanding example of a useful public relations display inspired by patriotism.

ADVERTISING AGENCY

Companies which advertise consistently use an advertising agency to help plan their program as well as prepare and place the copy. There is an established but curious practice in the business that enables a recognized advertising agency to handle its client's business and enjoy a 15 per cent discount on all the business so placed. Were the client to place the advertising directly with the newspaper or magazine, he would not be entitled to the discount. Hence the advertising agency can afford to give the client a good deal of service for the 15 per cent commission on all the copy it places.

The public relations director and his staff should work closely with the company's advertising department and the agency to make sure that their plans dovetail neatly. The public relations director, because of his over-all knowledge of company affairs and his professional training and experience in his field, is a valuable counselor to the advertising people. By the same token, when it comes to advertising a part of a public relations program, he should consult with the advertising man who may have the superior know-how and experience in the field.

A good public relations man must be a jack-of-all-trades and master of his own and he should never hesitate to seek advice from specialists in other fields.

DOES ADVERTISING PAY?

As has been suggested above, advertising may play a very important role in a public relations program. Before closing this chapter, however, we should note that advertising as a public relations tool has proven advantages as well as definite drawbacks. What are they?

Advantages

We can prepare our information exactly as we wish to have it disseminated. We are not dependent upon sympathetic treatment from the editor or rewrite man. Our entire message will be printed, spoken, or otherwise reproduced as we originally wrote it.

Our message may appear in newspapers and magazines as well as over radio or television networks of our own choice.

We do not have to "plant" a story and then sit back hoping and praying it will be used.

The timing of the message is completely within our control.

The same story may be put before the public several times, in exactly the same way or with a different approach.

We can pre-determine who shall receive our message.

In summary, we might say that when we use advertising as part of our public relations campaign, we can control the preparation, location, and timing of our message as well as the selection of its audience.

Drawbacks

Although an efficient means of reaching people, advertising is expensive and if our public relations budget is limited, we may not be able to afford it.

When our message appears as an advertisement, the public suspects it has received prejudiced treatment by the company and the reader may not be convinced. The same message, when printed as a news item, has every appearance of being an unprejudiced story since the public does not realize what a vast quantity of news is "planted."

Advertising can seldom do the job alone, and there is a danger that if we place too much reliance on advertising to accomplish our objective, we may overlook or ignore other and possibly more effective public relations tools that are at our command.

CHAPTER

6

Become a Public Relations Sleuth

Has your curiosity been piqued? Do you want to learn more about public relations? We certainly hope so, for new and interesting discoveries await you in the next section where you will see for yourself how public relations serves business, government, trade associations, social services, and education.

Of course you have not yet made up your mind about public relations, particularly since you have only read less than a third of this book! May we suggest, though, that you will find it fun, as well as stimulating and good training too, if you become an amateur public relations detective as you work, play, read, or carry on your normal everyday activities. You will be amazed to find how much of your life is surrounded by some facet of public relations, and playing Sherlock Holmes for a while may help you to evaluate the profession better. Here is how you can go about it.

When you read your newspaper, try to distinguish those stories and pictures which are "planted" from those which are not. Here are some clues to "planted" stories: news about the activities of any organization, group, government agency or company; news about new inventions or scientific discoveries; statements ascribed to government officials or company executives (they may, of course, be the result of a press conference held by a government agency or corporation); personnel appointments, shifts or advancements; financial and real estate news; social items and obituaries. Similarly "planted" pictures include those of new products, new factories, spectacular accomplishments of industry, newly appointed executives, famous personalities arriving at airports or railroad terminals (submitted by the carrier to get publicity for itself and not for the person photographed!), movie stars and starlets, bathing beauties and such. So much for free publicity that finds its way into the press, the radio, and television too.

You will get a real kick, however, from carefully watching the genuine news columns for stories that involve real public relations problems—stories about strikes, plant closings, failure of a product or service, dishonest employees, illegal corporate activities, fatal accidents to employees or the public, and the like. When you see this type of situation, pretend that you are the public relations man who has to handle the problem and work out your solution for re-establishing good public relations. Follow the development of your "case" and see if it is ultimately solved to your satisfaction.

Here is an example of what we mean, a story that started with a routine application for a license to erect a sign and ended on the editorial pages of the New York *Times* and the New York *Herald Tribune*—all within a very short period of time.

The National Sugar Refining Company of New York planned to erect a large illuminated advertising sign across the river from the United Nations Headquarters and adjacent to similar signs. Although it obtained the necessary legal permission, so much opposition was voiced by the United Nations and those who feared it would detract from the

United Nations surroundings, that the president of the sugar refining company stated he was impressed by "the evidence of public interest in beautifying the city's industrial waterfront." He thereupon canceled plans for building the sign and offered to contribute $2,500 toward a study to determine what industry could do to beautify the river. It was obvious to any student of public relations who followed the story as it unfolded that the company would have reaped much ill will had it proceeded with its original plans. But no one could have anticipated the unexpected financial offer which the company made and which earned for it laudatory editorials in two of the nation's leading newspapers—a feather in the cap of any public relations man!

When listening to the radio or enjoying movies or television, watch for product "identifications" or company "mentions" which are the fruit of an energetic publicity campaign. Companies are spending more and more time and effort cooperating with television and movie producers in an effort to reap the best possible publicity harvest. You may smile with satisfaction when you spot the results of their efforts.

Read your mail carefully and see if you can detect the clever work of the public relations director behind the text of your business correspondence. Watch the next political campaign and judge for yourself the public relations sense exhibited by each of the candidates.

And as you walk down the street, your ever-alert eye will watch for merchants and business concerns that are public relations conscious. You will see it in little things, such as a ramp to make it easy for mothers with baby carriages to get into the store, a roadside sign in good taste, a hand cart for the convenience of customers who must carry packages from the store to their car, a sign in a drugstore reading "24-hour service—our telephone never sleeps," another sign in the window of the snack bar: "Our waitresses enjoy serving you;

they do not expect gratuities," a shoe store that hangs polishing cloths out front so people can wipe their shoes, etc.

A little knowledge may be a dangerous thing but in your case it can add to the spice of living, enable you to look behind the scenes, and add to your own storehouse of information about the world of public relations which surrounds you.

Try it. Start today!

PART 2

PUBLIC RELATIONS AT YOUR SERVICE

CHAPTER

7

Public Relations in Business

Like millions of other Americans you have probably pushed back the familiar red door to enter one of the two thousand stores that still bear the name of the man who opened the first "five and ten cent store"—F. W. Woolworth. To you or the average customer it is just another business. But is it? Read what the company says about public relations in its 1953 report to its shareholders:

"Woolworth's is much more than an organization of nearly 2,000 retail stores housing a vast array of high-value merchandise.

"Woolworth's is people.

"The effective base of the whole Woolworth operation is the relation with the individual customer and the community in which the customer lives. . . .

"Tens of thousands of employees, who are loyal to Woolworth's and devoted to the welfare of the home community, are Woolworth's most effective representatives at the community level, although the store manager officially represents the Company.

". . . In the conduct of day to day operations, the Woolworth Company is ever mindful of its responsibilities to the employees, to the customers and communities it serves, and hence to the individual stockholders.

"Woolworth's is people." (Emphasis is ours)

This is the clue to the approach business takes toward public relations. Every business enterprise is "people," for it deals with four groups of individuals:

Shareholders—the people who own the business
Employees—the people who run the business, make and sell the product or service
Customers—the people who buy the product or service
Community—the people who are neighbors of the business

In reaching or dealing with each of these groups, public relations becomes the keystone of the policy adopted by the management. In most companies the public relations department is charged with the over-all responsibility not only for handling the publicity and giving out information about the company, but for assisting in the formation of public relations policies. In practice the public relations department cannot go down into each department and do the public relations job for it. But it can and does suggest and help.

Here is where the responsibility lies with each of the above groups for carrying out the public relations policy:

Shareholders—Corporate Secretary's Office and/or Public Relations
Employees—Personnel or Labor Relations Director
Customers—General Sales Manager
Community—Local Sales Manager or Plant Manager

Shareholders

For the benefit of readers not familiar with how American corporate democracy works, an individual who has invested money in a company, whether it be a few dollars or several million, becomes a stockholder—or shareholder—and receives shares of stock evidencing his part ownership of the enterprise. Each share of stock entitles him to one vote in the election of directors, appointment of auditors, and such other matters as may be put to a vote. The shareholders elect the board of directors who in turn select and elect the officers—or management. The directors are charged with the over-all responsibility of guiding the company, but since they usually are men engaged in other business or professional pursuits, they leave the day to day direction of the company to the officers (management).

One of the most bitter and best-publicized battles for control of a corporation was fought in 1954 when Robert Young, wealthy head of the Allegheny Corporation and a large stockholder of the New York Central Railroad, was refused a seat on the board of directors of the railroad. Thereupon he publicly declared his intent to upset the management and win control of the company. Going before the shareholders (numbering over 40,000 individuals) he asked them to elect his slate of directors, including himself as Chairman of the Board. The battle was waged in the press and through letters to the shareholders, each side extolling its own virtues and smearing its opponents.

At first the management expected to win without any difficulty but as the fight proceeded it became evident that Young was picking up votes. He won because enough owners were more impressed with what he promised them than with the performance of the management. It was a death blow to the New York Central management and the various business and banking interests which had long held directorships in that company. Perhaps even more important, it was a sharp warning to every corporation executive whose company's stocks were widely held by the public. It could happen to them too because "people are business" and the owners of the business, not the management, are the people who decide, through their proxy vote, who will manage it.

For years the shareholder has been the forgotten man. There is a saying down on Wall Street about shareholders that goes like this: "Don't send them anything unless it's a dividend check." Most managements thought that as long as they paid dividends they could forget the owners. Today every intelligent president knows that the best way to stay in office is to keep the owners informed and as happy as possible so that if it is necessary to reduce or eliminate dividend payments, the owners will understand, be patient and not immediately support a change in management. Most enlightened companies have shareholder relations programs—public relations programs for shareholders. These are usually carried out by the secretary of the corporation who ordinarily coordinates them with the over-all policy of the public relations department.

Employees

In the final analysis it is the employee who expresses to the shareholder, his fellow employees, the customers and the community the spirit of his company's public relations policy. "Business is people," and whether or not the employee likes it, his company will in some way or other be judged by the way he behaves and the things for which he stands. He is therefore encouraged to be a good citizen, to enter into community and civic activities, to attend church, to vote, etc.

You may say that an employee is free to live as he pleases after his work is done. He *is,* but as a loyal employee who is interested in the growth and success of his company, he has added reason to be a good citizen since he is a representative of his employer. "Business is people," and one of the best ways a business can be a good citizen is to have its employees conduct themselves as good citizens.

A company cannot adequately discharge its obligations to the community merely by writing a check. More than money is required and expected. The active help of the people who constitute the business is essential if the company is to be looked upon as a good citizen.

General Foods moved its headquarters offices from New York City to the nearby suburban city of White Plains. On the day the new office opened, Charles G. Mortimer, president of the company, spoke briefly to the employees telling them why the company had moved and what it hoped to accomplish in its new quarters. The following excerpts from his address point up the responsibilities of the employee:

". . . Let me call your attention to the fact that White Plains did not invite us to come here; we invited ourselves. In a sense, then, we are guests here—until we *earn* the right to be called neighbors.

". . . In White Plains we will be a big company, and one of the largest employers in the city. We will be watched, I suspect in some ways critically, but also hopefully, for the people of White Plains know that we have come to stay. What we *do* will speak far louder than what we *say*.

"Our cue as good citizens, as well as GF people, is to enter into the activities—and shoulder the responsibilities—of the area we have moved into, in a way which will cause our neighbors to say among themselves, 'Those General Foods people are certainly the right kind of folks. We're happy that they moved out here.' "

Just as every coin has two sides, so has this matter of employee relations. We have touched on the employee's responsibility to the community as a representative of his company. Management in turn has a responsibility to the employee—not only to provide him with the best possible working conditions and opportunity to grow personally and prosper with the company, but also to have a sense of belonging and a maximum of self-respect. It is in this area that it is most important to remember "Business is people," but it is surprising how many managements which have excellent public relations policies and departments for dealing with the public (shareholders, customers, and community) completely overlook the fact that their own employees are people too and that they deserve the same type of consideration and treatment which is lavished on the public.

Two important parts of an employee relations program which are the responsibility of most public relations departments are: (1) handling all publicity in connection with personnel or labor relations, and (2) editing the company house organ (magazine for employees). Both of these functions call for very close coordination and cooperation between the public relations and personnel (or labor relations) departments. In addition the public relations department may also be called upon to conduct or participate in one or more of the following activities: periodic open houses and/or Christmas parties for employees and their families, employee outings and picnics, indoctrination program for new employees, special training films, annual report for employees.

A company should have a well-planned employee relations program in order to keep its employees happy, informed, loyal, and eager to increase production and sales. The conduct of employee relations is becoming a specialty of its own. Although it operates according to the same basic principles as public relations, there are many complicating factors, such as labor agreements, wage and salary schedules, seniority rules, union rules, and federal or state labor laws. To plan and carry out an effective employee relations program one should have some firsthand knowledge of these matters because they affect the implementation of any plan.

Employee relations—or labor relations as it is more often called—is an excellent field for the man or woman who has had training and experience in public relations and is temperamentally suited to this more exacting kind of work. It offers a variety of job opportunities in a comparatively new field.

Customers

Attending a recent convention of life insurance agents at one of the country's most exclusive resort hotels, was a man who brought his wife and two children. One noon as he strolled through the magnificent lobby, he noticed water dripping through the ceiling and porters frantically trying to cover or move the expensive period furniture. When he reached the corridor leading to his room, which was directly over the lobby, he was horrified to discover water gushing out from beneath the door of his bedroom.

Suddenly, he remembered explaining to his twelve-year-old boy how the sprinkler nozzle that protruded from the ceiling would go into action if a fire produced enough heat to melt the metal bar that held the valve shut. Sure enough, his inquisitive son had climbed on top of the bureau and taken a lighted candle and a pitcher to catch what he expected would be a trickle of water—but the unexpected flood waters were let loose.

After a miserable lunch our friend received the dreaded summons to appear in the manager's office. Knowing full well he could never begin to pay for the damage, he went prepared for the worst. The manager asked him to take a seat, then said:

"Mr. Hibbard, we apologize for the great inconvenience to which you and your family have been put. May I ask you a favor? Would you please gather together all your clothes that have been water-soaked and call the valet? We have arranged with the laundry to have everything back to you in perfect condition by six o'clock. Naturally, there will be no charge for this. One thing more—we are also arranging to move you to more comfortable rooms and hope you will overlook this extra trouble. Thank you."

If you are looking for an example of good customer relations, this is it!

The customer makes or breaks any business. We therefore find an interesting relationship between public relations and customer relations. First, consider the four steps a salesman must take every time he makes a sale: he must get the prospect's *attention*, he must arouse his *interest*, he must make him *desire* the product or service, and then he must lead him to *make a decision* to buy.

What influences the prospect's *decision* to say yes and thereby become a customer? True, the persuasion of the salesman is important but the best salesman in the world cannot obtain a favorable decision if the prospect does not think well of the company. He has already been influenced by the company's advertising, the reputation it has established for its products or service, and by the over-all public opinion of the company. You can therefore see that the kind of public relations job that has been accomplished may have great bearing on the customer's decision to buy.

Under the direction of its hard-working and imaginative public relations director, Bob Barbour, the Jersey Central Railroad has given the lie to any general assertion that railroads don't care about their customers. Working out revised commutation schedules with groups representing towns along the line, installing a system of colored lights at Jersey City terminal to tell passengers quickly the destinations of trains, informing station agents when trains are late so they can tell anxious wives of commuters, installing a large projector in the New York ferry terminal to inform passengers of train delays, emergencies, etc., leaving bulletins on seats for passengers, and sparking a new brand of customer courtesy, are but some of the results of Barbour's activities. Don't you agree that these are unusually good customer relations, particularly since railroads don't make a dime from commuters?

Perhaps the department store evidences the strongest belief in good customer relations. What other business extends so many courtesies and conveniences to its customers? The modern store furnishes its patrons free parking, free delivery of purchases, charge accounts, time installment plans, the privilege of returning merchandise, personal shopping service, advance notice of special sales, restaurant, post office, beauty parlor, photographic studio, and other services. It is true you will find that the service type of business appears to be more customer relations conscious than the manufacturer of a product. However, there are many companies, manufacturing drab or unexciting items, that are keenly aware of the importance of good customer relations, but the nature of their business does not lend itself to colorful or elaborate programs.

Community

What would you think if an officer of the country's largest savings bank took your arm and ushered you into a spacious room where a group of girls and boys were watching a movie, drinking cokes, and discussing their version of community leadership? You might well wonder what banking had come to but such activities are merely a regular part of the Bowery Savings Bank's community relations program conducted in the main office opposite Grand Central Terminal and in another office located on the original site of the bank—in the heart of New York City's famous Bowery.

Chester W. Schmidt, the bank's vice-president in charge of developing and guiding its community relations program, explained to us how the "Junior Advisors" were started. Anxious to build public acceptance for the bank and show that the bank recognizes its responsibility to share in local community affairs, it was found that a youth leadership training program was badly needed and that the bank could make its best contribution by undertaking such a program among the neighborhood junior high school students. Under the program worked out by Mr. Schmidt and his staff, the students are (1) acquainted with a savings bank's role in the community, (2) taught the importance of thrift, (3) inspired with basic leadership training, and (4) it is hoped, convinced that the bank and its friendly staff stand ready to be of real service to the community.

This community relations program is paying off to the bank through better understanding of the bank by the community, increased school savings accounts, and general employee enthusiasm for the project, which has done much to improve morale. The bank has also used every opportunity to tell others about the program, for this is public relations at its best and bears much telling.

Mr. Schmidt believes that his unusual background helped to qualify him for the job. "I was born a Lutheran, educated in Catholic schools and university, and always lived in predominantly Jewish communities. I know and understand the people in the communities our bank serves. There was nothing unusual about the Bowery area to me, because people are essentially the same everywhere. My job is to make the bank acceptable to the community."

Starting his banking career as a clerk, Mr. Schmidt later supervised the installation of the new punched-card system as he worked his way up to the executive rank. With his assignment to community relations, he immediately plunged into community activities, volunteering his time and services to many organizations. In spite of his broad working knowledge of banking and community relations, Mr. Schmidt is always on the alert lest he "get into a corner." By this he means that in community relations people should not narrow their activity or interest to a single area lest they lose sight of the over-all problems and the relationships between the local community and the larger one of which it is but a part. The list of civic, eduational, and welfare organizations in which he is an active member is proof that Mr. Schmidt will never run the danger of getting himself "into a corner."

Little wonder when the Bowery Savings Bank undertook to expand into the heart of Harlem that Chester Schmidt was selected to become manager of the new office. Long before its scheduled opening, Mr. Schmidt was working hard to establish contacts in the community, laying plans for a "Junior Advisor" program in the area to be served by the bank, and preparing community opinion for favorable acceptance by listening carefully to their expectations.

"Personal contacts pay off every time," Mr. Schmidt insists. "You don't win community approval by offering prizes or rewards. You do it by rolling up your sleeves and working on the community's problems, and by bringing the youngsters to the bank. There through personal contact they learn to trust and understand us.

"Remember, though," Mr. Schmidt warned, "community relations is a two-way educational process. Not only does it require participation in community affairs to build acceptance of your business in the community, but sometimes there is the problem of building acceptance of a community within the organization. All of us are biased or prejudiced to some extent and not infrequently many biased objections to a plan must be overcome successfully before it can win approval and be implemented."

Other Examples of Community Relations

When General Motors dedicated the Buick-Oldsmobile-Pontiac Assembly Division plant at Arlington, Texas, in 1954, Mr. Harlow H. Curtice, president of the corporation, said:

"We sincerely hope that with this new plant we shall be able to contribute substantially to your further progress. It is our wish—and intention—to become a constructive part of your community and to contribute importantly to its civic and cultural life as well as to its economic life. In other words, we intend to be a good industrial citizen."

As a community service many companies feel an obligation to assist with fund raising drives by making available personnel or facilities in addition to contributing money.

Government often makes demands on industry for men of outstanding executive ability. At the request of President Eisenhower, industrial leaders like George M. Humphrey of the M. A. Hanna Company, Harold E. Talbott of the Talbott Company, and Charles Wilson and Roger Kyes of General Motors Corporation were released by their managements and entered their country's service, causing great personal sacrifice to themselves and loss of important leadership to their companies.

Many public relations departments prepare and distribute handbooks for the guidance of sales and plant managers in dealing with the press and the various community contacts. Preparation of such a book forces the management to sit down and agree upon its over-all public relations plans as they affect its shareholders, employees, customers and the community.

Chamber of Commerce bodies which exist in almost every city or town of good size promote the economic and social welfare of the community. They conduct a continuing community relations program aimed not only at their own citizens but at people residing outside the community. Convention bureaus, boards of trade, development councils and similar organizations all create good will in and out of the community with the end purpose of boosting business, increasing employment, and insuring greater prosperity for the community.

To Summarize

Business is people and deals with owners, employers, customers, and neighbors. Progressive business leaders recognize that success depends on the favorable opinion of each of these groups toward the business.

Success in business doesn't just happen. It is the result of good planning, hard work, quality production, and a happy relationship between the company and the four types of people with whom it comes in contact.

A sound public relations program is one of the best ways of achieving this happy relationship. It is a mutual responsibility of the public relations department, management, and employees to join hands in carrying out a public relations program that will present the company in the best possible light to its owners, customers and neighbors.

CHAPTER

8

Public Relations in Government

You might suspect that government presents few opportunities for men and women who are anxious to practice public relations. But wait a minute! Our Federal government is the largest employer in the world and when you also consider the forty-eight states, the innumerable cities, and the newly created public authorities that dot the nation, you have uncovered a wealth of opportunity.

This is such a large field we can only hope to skim the surface and suggest a few of the possibilities that exist. First, it might be helpful to list the chief reasons why so many government agencies have provided for a public relations staff—or information service—as it is more often called in the Federal government.

A public relations program may be designed for one or more of the following reasons:

1. To keep the taxpayer informed about the services performed or available for his use.
2. To interest citizens in their government and help them better to understand and appraise what it does.
3. To win popular support for new legislation or reforms.

4. To gain public approval for an agency and thus insure its staying in business.
5. To provide for the public a means of contacting the top people who run an agency.

FEDERAL GOVERNMENT

Thousands of employees are needed to staff the information and public relations staffs of the numerous administrative agencies, the military public relations projects and the State Department's foreign information program.

The Military

The armed forces have a particularly difficult public relations problem during peace time. No one wants to serve in the army or foot the bills. In a democracy like ours, there is little sympathy or interest in military matters when the danger of war is not imminent. However, defense is our nation's largest business and will probably continue to be so. Therefore, there will be a continuous need for an effective public relations program that (1) aims at making an army career attractive to our young men, (2) shows the taxpayer he is getting value received for his dollar spent, and (3) keeps the nation informed about the true state of its offensive and defensive might. The magnitude of the job is indicated by an estimate the Secretary of Defense made during the fiscal year 1952 when he stated that over 3,800 uniformed and civilian employees were handling advertising, publicity, and public relations for the Department of Defense.

Information Specialists

From time to time the U.S. Civil Service Commission lists openings for Information Specialists in the *press field*, the *magazine and publications field*, and the *radio field* to search out and write factual material about the activities of Federal agencies which would be of concern to farmers, businessmen, working men, and the general public. In the *motion picture field* scripts for scenarios involving action taken by Federal agencies are written and edited, whereas in the *visual field* pictorial material, such as photos, posters, slide films, etc., are prepared to support narrative presentations of facts about actions taken by a Federal agency. In the *attitudes and opinions field* opinions which have been expressed by columnists, editorial writers, or radio commentators are carefully read and digested to guide the operating officials of agencies which are carrying out programs directed by Congress. In *public liason* requests for program assistance, background information, and speakers are handled. Such requests come from all parts of the country and from all types of organizations. Information Specialists to perform other types of work are sought from time to time.

There are openings too for Information and Educational Clerks to do fact finding, for Information and Editorial Clerks to do writing, for Information Clerks, Editorial Clerks, Indexing Clerks, Proofreading Clerks, etc. These positions naturally call for less experience than Information Specialists, and education may count heavily in place of experience for those applicants who have done college and/or postgraduate work.

Full information on these and other government jobs is available from the U.S. Civil Service Commission, Washington 25, D.C.

United States Information Agency

According to the *United States Government Organization Manual* "the purpose of the United States Information Agency, as stated in a directive from the National Security Council, is to submit evidence to the peoples of other nations by means of communications techniques, that the objectives and policies of the United States are in harmony with and advance their legitimate aspirations for freedom, progress, and peace." In other words, the agency explains the objectives of the United States and brings to other nations information about all aspects of life and culture of the people of the United States. The fact that this *one* agency maintains field offices in over 150 cities located all over the world is indicative of its size.

The Press Service (which is just one of its services) acquires and furnishes or produces press materials, pamphlets, magazines and photo services to the overseas posts of the U.S. Information Service and provides technical direction concerning the use of these products.

According to A. W. von Strube of the Bureau of Census' Public Information Office: "Public information offices in the various government departments and bureaus are generally staffed with people who have had experience in newspaper work or other media.

"Young people aspiring toward this type of government career will be well-advised, therefore, not only to choose their college courses toward this end, but to expect to build up a background of news experience before entering government service."

STATE GOVERNMENT

A survey made in 1951 showed that 700 public relations and information men and women were employed in 43 states at an estimated annual salary cost of $4,000,000. No doubt this number has increased greatly since that time, for many state governments are finding it desirable to publicize their good deeds to dollar-conscious citizens and taxpayers.

The Indiana Plan

One of the most unusual examples of public relations undertaken by a state government was the series of Governmental Service Conferences conceived by Governor Ralph F.

Gates of Indiana after his inauguration in January 1945. Various cities were selected to be "state capital for a day" and top state officials conducted a series of conferences and meetings with residents of that part of the state. Heads of about eighteen departments were chosen to participate and explain the work of their agency to the large audiences that flocked to the meetings. During the morning, classes were held for high school seniors, afternoons were given over to a round-table conference with local officials, labor representatives, civic groups, etc., and the night dinner meeting featured an open forum at which the department heads were available to answer questions fired at them from the audience. This was a courageous and strenuous undertaking but one that doubtless won great popular support for the new administration.

Hi-Ho, Come to the Fair!

If you think that agencies of a state government do not offer interesting possibilities for a public relations career, then meet Foster Potter. He is director of public relations for the New York State Department of Agriculture and Markets. It sounded rather dull to us too; we imagined Mr. Potter singing the praises of New York State cheddar cheese or making a good-will visit to New York City's Fulton Fish Market. But were we wrong! Listen to Mr. Potter's story as he tells it himself.

"You asked me how I got into public relations. It was because I was born almost on a fair grounds. Across the street from the entrance to the Chenango County Fair at Norwich, New York, that is. Fair people roomed at our house. I've never seen an act half as thrilling as that of the Flying Lady who occupied our back bedroom. She hasn't anything to do with our story except that I've never been able to figure out how she soared through the air against a black background in her tent. Or why the man who raffled 'canaries' by spinning a wheel should give me one when he knew that in a couple of weeks the yellow dye would wear off and we'd have a sparrow in the house.

"Circuses showed on the fair grounds every summer. How could I ever forget William F. Cody swinging up our front sidewalk and taking me over to sit beside him during the matinee of 'Buffalo Bill's Wild West Show'? My father was a train dispatcher. He had gone out of his way to do something to get Buffalo Bill's circus train through to Norwich on time. Mr. Cody wanted to know what he could do to repay him. My seat of honor and the envy of every kid in town, was the measure of Buffalo Bill's gratitude.

"I gravitated into newspaper work in high school, spent a little time on a ship in World War I, went to a college at Syracuse and also newspapered on the Syracuse *Herald*, a relationship that was to last fifteen years. In all that time I suppose it was only natural that my beat included the New York State Fair at Syracuse.

"So in 1934 when the paper had to retrench to stay in business, it meant the air for 11 reporters. A wink and a gasp later I was on the State Fair payroll in charge of all its publicity, the State Fair being one of the enterprises of this State Department.

"With the Fair ended, the Commissioner of Agriculture and Markets suggested continuing the relationship. He foresaw six months a year building good will and customers for the State Fair and the other six months cementing Department relations with the county fairs' managements. What he didn't foresee was the shift in the political complexion of the Legislature that year-end.

"The new administration back there in 1935 decided that the Department as a whole was in need of a public relations program—one of the first such in the New York State government. Well, twenty years and World War II later, I am still here and the State Fair is still one of the big activities, although we now employ an agency to do most of that promotion work, and a man who devotes all his time to public relations work with the county fairs.

"As an avocation I'm also public relations director of the Altamont (N.Y.) Tri-County Fair. The present board of that Fair took over a run-down, discredited organization and in just a few years has built it up to the third largest county fair attendance in the State with a reputation that's gaining unbelievably.

"It could be that the other fellow's pasture always looks a little greener. Certainly the money to be made in public relations is not in government. It's in industry. The only trouble is that industry doesn't operate any fairs. But industrial public relations is a wide open field. It should present the most interesting challenge possible to a young person going into public relations. I've just one word of advice. Don't miss an opportunity to learn every device in the world in the art of public speaking. The persuasive kind, of course. Then use it."

Not everyone doing public relations for an agency of a state finds his work as completely satisfying as Mr. Potter. However his experience shows that a person can expand a hobby or special interest into a full-time vocation. Perhaps your hobby can lead you to a happy and useful career in public relations too!

Of all state agencies probably the one that needs to cultivate the best public relations—and has the hardest time doing so—is the Department of Taxation and Finance. Norman Gallman is director of publications and public relations for the New York State Department of Taxation and Finance, a position which you can readily see keeps him busy. Mr. Gallman came to the State with a good newspaper background, having started as a reporter-printer on the *Allegany County Democrat*. He transferred to the editorship of the Allegany County edition of the *Hornell Tribune* and then spent eight years as news editor of the *Wellsville Daily Reporter*. Appointed State motor vehicle information secretary in 1938, he became tax publications editor the following year and director of publications and public relations in 1943, all assignments being within the Department of Taxation and Finance.

"As to background and training," Mr. Gallman said, "I belong to the school which regards actual newspaper experience over a period of years as the first and foremost requirement for a career in public relations.

"I have known a few topflight public relations men who came into the business from other fields. But by far the largest number of good public relations men in my acquaintance had previous long and varied experiences in the newspaper profession."

CITIES

Cities too are public relations conscious because urban dwellers can readily judge the accomplishments of their municipal government. Many cities and towns issue an annual report of their activities and finances which is distributed to every home. A few are even using movies, radio, or TV to inform their citizens of what they are doing.

A Successful Bond Issue

The town of South Boston, Virginia, used an effective public relations program to obtain approval of certain bond issues. The mayor and members of the council visited every civic group to explain the importance of the issues. Several spot announcements were recorded by members of the council and other radio programs were arranged. The help of local newspapers and civic organizations was also enlisted. Every home received an attractive booklet with eye-catching illustrations explaining the whole affair. Such a thorough program assured approval of the project.

Airport Open House

The city of Toledo built a new airport at a cost of almost four million dollars. The building contractor thought it would be a fine idea to let the taxpayers inspect their new purchase and with permission of the city fathers placed news stories, radio plugs and half-page advertisements that invited Toledo motorists to drive their cars over the runways, taxi strips, and ramps of the 1,000-acre airport. More than 4,000 cars carrying some 15,000 people drove about the airport on the five-mile conducted tour. Today the citizens of Toledo are extra proud of their airport!

Model Ordinance

A model municipal public relations ordinance was drawn up in 1951 at the New School for Social Research in New York. As a guide for city councils planning a public relations department, this model provides for the establishment of a separate department or bureau in a city "to achieve a better understanding between the citizen and the city government." After listing the purposes of a public relations department, it spells out its duties and responsibilities.

PUBLIC AUTHORITIES

A new type of government agency—the authority—has recently become increasingly popular. An authority is usually established when some large public works or public improvement is to be undertaken. Under the direction of prominent business and civic leaders and backed by the credit of the state or city government which created it, a public authority may float bonds to obtain necessary capital to construct and operate the facility or facilities for which it was set up. Profits are used to pay off indebtedness and make additional improvements.

New York State Thruway

One of the more recently established authorities is the New York State Thruway Authority which built and now operates the thruway that extends from New York City to Buffalo. Robert M. Monahan is its director of public relations, coming to his assignment with a good newspaper background. A Notre Dame graduate, he held various positions and did free-lance writing before he entered the newspaper business in 1938 as New York State capital correspondent for the International News Service. A year later he joined the Albany staff of the United Press in a similar capacity and remained until his appointment to the Authority in 1950. During the construction stage of the thruway, Mr. Monahan's behind-the-scene direction might be detected in the excellent newspaper coverage given the project.

The Port of New York Authority

If your airplane should land at La Guardia, Idlewild, or Newark Airport, if your car should cross the Hudson River, passing through the graceful towers of the George Washington Bridge or scooting under the Hudson through the Holland or Lincoln tunnels to park finally on the roof of the giant new Union Bus Depot just off Times Square, you've used one or more of the many facilities of The Port of New York Authority. Freight, grain, bus and motor truck terminals, Port Newark, the Hoboken Port Authority piers, as well as three bridges connecting Staten Island with New Jersey are also responsibilities of this Authority which is headed by six commissioners from New York State and six from New

Jersey, appointed by their respective governors to serve without pay for terms of six years.

The Authority was created in 1921 as a self-supporting corporate agency to deal with planning and development of terminal and transportation facilities and to improve and protect the commerce of the Port District. One of the founders of the Authority said: "It is a three-legged stool. One leg is administration. The second leg is finance and engineering. The third leg, and one without which it cannot stand, is public relations." That statement is even truer today now that The Port of New York Authority operates so many diverse facilities. And to guide the public relations program the Authority chose one of the ablest women in the profession—Lee K. Jaffe—a tall woman whose black hair and well-chosen wardrobe accent her striking appearance.

Before most of us have our first date, Mrs. Jaffe was self-supporting, assisting her father in his business when she was twelve. "My first job for outsiders, undertaken the day after I graduated from Akron High School," she recalled, "was in a foreign exchange bank. I was hired as a stenographer but I wasn't a stenographer and I had to deliver a better job than was expected of me in order to hold the job."

Here is an important clue to Mrs. Jaffe's success in business. She always went beyond her assignments—not because she was aggressive or ambitious, but rather because she was curious, and anxious to avoid boredom. This philosophy paid off later in Washington where she worked her way up to become secretary to a United States senator who also owned one of the largest papers in the Middle West. After the senator sold the paper and retired from office, the new owners asked her to be their Washington correspondent. When she protested that she was in no way familiar with the job, they wired back: "What do you think you have been doing for us all along?" They were referring to the errands she had been running for them on Capitol Hill, getting answers to their questions about Washington affairs. Thus she became a reporter starting at the very top of the ladder as a Washington correspondent.

Marriage interrupted her newspaper career and brought her to New York City. It was fortunate that she quickly mastered the art of keeping house because the day after Pearl Harbor she felt it her patriotic duty to accept an urgent invitation to handle publicity in the local Civil Defense organization at City Hall. From here she went to the Office of War Information, assigned to O.P.A. as its information officer, the lone woman holding this office in the country-wide setup. When domestic O.W.I. was liquidated, she transferred to the Office of Price Administration as regional radio director. In 1944 she left the O.P.A. to go with The Port of New York Authority as assistant director of public relations. There being no director, her title was soon changed to recognize her for what she was in fact.

When asked for her definition of public relations, Mrs. Jaffe thought for a moment, then said she would like to paraphrase *Fortune* magazine's definition of business public relations in order to apply it to government. Here is how she put it: "Good government public relations is good performance publicly appreciated. It is a democratic way of life. Government must first do a job that people can think well of, and then intelligently and deftly call attention to it. There is no magic to our formula for achieving a good public relations program. We simply add an honest and efficient information service to honest and efficient administration of a public service program. The result is informed confidence and respect."

The Port Authority respects public relations as a top level function and Mrs. Jaffe is at all times aware of policy and is consulted during its formation. Because the press knows of this, her statements are accepted as official and informed and all contacts with the press are handled by her office. "We make every effort to help newspapers get their stories," Mrs. Jaffe said. "Special inspection trips to our various facilities and press previews of new facilities have been greatly appreciated and constitute an important part of our public relations program." Mrs. Jaffe prefers to furnish written stories to the press rather than hold press conferences because it saves time for the reporters and her staff too. Her releases attempt to answer every question that might be asked on the story. Press releases of The Port Authority are never press agent stunts or personality build-ups. Thus, when a newspaper receives a press release from The Port Authority it knows that it will contain news and invariably it will print the story.

The favorable press enjoyed by The Port of New York Authority is indicated forcefully by the fact that in the past ten years there have been almost 2,500 editorials in the metropolitan Port District papers supporting The Port Authority.

FOREIGN GOVERNMENTS

Foreign governments have a story to tell, for they are anxious to curry the favor of the American businessman and tourist. Many governments have established information and travel agencies in various cities of the United States to assist Americans in obtaining needed information about their country as well as to entice them to make a visit. Some of these agencies do extensive advertising and publicity to call attention to the charms of the fatherland.

Vive La France!

One last proof we must offer to those who still suspect that working for a government may prove dull or routine. Imagine an orchestra softly playing "I Love Paris in the Spring," then allow us to introduce you to American-born Norman Reader, public information director of the French Government Tourist Office in New York.

Mr. Reader's office was re-established in 1946 when a mere 50,000 Americans made a trip to France. In 1954 more than 350,000 journeyed abroad to visit La Belle France, thanks to the persistent efforts of Mr. Reader and his staff to tell their fellow countrymen about the joys of traveling in France. It was estimated that during the year 1951, 300,000 of us succumbed to Mr. Reader's invitation and dropped a hundred million American dollars into the French economy, the largest single source of badly needed dollars. No wonder that although French governments come and go, the Tourist Office goes on forever!

Mr. Reader says: "I suppose my own public relations start goes back to when I realized for the first time, around the age of ten, that words did curious things to me. From this initial stirring sprang long excursions into the world of books and the gradual emergence of an urge to put things down on paper. I have satisfied my urge to scribble and learned to fashion the kind of material that newspapers, magazines, radio, and television find interesting and useful. I have learned the public relations trade through actual experience rather than by formal education, and certainly had I been ill-equipped temperamentally, I'd not be sitting where I am at the moment."

He began his career writing feature stories for the motion-picture industry. At Uncle Sam's request he became a private in the Air Force but it was not long before he was appointed public relations officer of the First Air Force, in which capacity he was responsible for the direction and maintenance of public relations activities of more than twenty-five fighter and bomber bases stretching from Maine to Florida. He was active in introducing the public to the famous P-47 Thunderbolt and the fast A-26 fighter planes.

Joining the re-activated French Government Tourist Office as public information director in 1946, Mr. Reader has since concentrated on bettering Franco-American relations by instituting a sound program of public relations, advertising, and many newsworthy promotions. One of his outstanding promotions, marking the 2,000th birthday of Paris, included a junket of famous French chefs to the Chambord Restaurant in New York and the visit of a New Jersey girl to the traditional celebration of "Bourgeois Evening" in Paris.

The New York headquarters staff consists of fifteen people, and in addition six branches are located in principal cities. Obviously the purpose of the Tourist Office is to stimulate interest in travel to France by making available information and promoting the country through advertising, radio programs, films, attractive folders, maps, booklets, and special promotions. One unique service which Mr. Reader's office offers the press is a monthly clip sheet presenting stories and pictures of French tourist attractions and details of coming events in the world of music, art, drama, and religious festivals. Specially trained staff members are available to help the public plan every detail of their trips.

Here is the philosophy that Norman Reader has adopted toward public relations: "Chiefly because of temperament, I have gravitated toward a middle-of-the-road approach to public relations. I have found that a natural indolence plus an instinct for theatrics have helped give my public relations operation a happy balance that has not only kept me at peace with myself and off the psychiatrist's couch, but also led me along paths that some have been kind enough to label success."

In Conclusion

The various and sundry government agencies offer innumerable job opportunities for those interested in practicing public relations or one of its related activities. The pay is generally below that offered by private industry and opportunity for advancement may be more limited because of civil service requirements. However, a degree of security, not found outside governmental circles, helps to compensate for these disadvantages. Of the two, private industry offers more lucrative, exciting and diverse opportunities—but with less job security.

CHAPTER

9

How Public Relations Serves Social Agencies

"Brother, Can You Spare a Dime?" was the title of a popular song during the depression days of the 1930's. Today, men are no longer seen behind pathetic street stands selling apples, families are not being dispossessed for failure to make mortgage payments, and unemployment is not the serious problem it was then. Nevertheless, there is a continuing need for funds to help the poor, care for the sick, and carry on medical research, as well as for many other worthwhile causes—all dedicated to making life better.

1. *HEALTH AGENCIES*

As medical science succeeds in discovering and isolating certain diseases, it then becomes possible for specialized research groups to study each in order to find the cause and remedy. Afflictions such as cerebral palsy, multiple sclerosis, and paraplegia, to name but a few, were hardly known twenty-five years ago. Today, thanks to expert diagnosis, it is possible to identify positively and treat many diseases which formerly baffled the doctors. The need for research in fields like those mentioned above, plus heart disease, cancer, arthritis, and many others, is critical. It is fortunate that each year the public responds by donating millions of dollars to organizations devoted to eradicating disease.

Such organizations should, if successful, work themselves out of a job! Take tuberculosis, for instance. The famous Trudeau Sanatorium at Saranac Lake, New York, closed its doors on its 70th anniversary because advances in the treatment of tuberculosis made it unnecessary to continue its operation. Once a dread killer, TB is gradually being wiped out because new drugs help in its cure, and the continual program of education that urges people to have annual chest X-rays has substantially cut down the number of the afflicted. The need for local tuberculosis organizations will continue, of course, although their importance will diminish as the spotlight swings to other diseases that await solution.

To get a picture of how public relations serves a health agency, let's look in on one of the largest and perhaps best known, the National Foundation for Infantile Paralysis, which was founded in 1938 by the late President Franklin D. Roosevelt.

Probably the biggest job of educating the public ever undertaken by a national health agency was tackled in 1954 by the National Foundation for Infantile Paralysis when the Polio Vaccine Trials were introduced in various parts of the country. A Gallup poll shows 90 per cent of the people in the United States knew about the trials—more than know the full name of the President!

In 217 areas, 25,000,000 people had to be told about an experiment that could not be called an experiment. A vast army of workers—200,000 lay volunteers, 20,000 doctors, 10,000 nurses, 14,000 school principals and 50,000 classroom teachers had to be recruited as volunteers to assist in giving injections to some 650,000 children. Parental fear that the vaccine might prove harmful to *their* child had to be allayed.

Was ever a public relations department faced with such a

task? We doubt it, but the fact that the trials were so successful was in large measure due to the work of Miss Dorothy Ducas, director of public relations, and her experienced staff.

A former student of Connecticut College for Women and a graduate of Columbia School of Journalism, Miss Ducas was the youngest winner of a Pulitzer Traveling Scholarship at that time. In addition to establishing herself as a free-lance writer for many leading magazines, Miss Ducas worked successively for the New York *Herald Tribune*, New York *Evening Post*, *McCall's* magazine, International News Service, *This Week* magazine, *Woman's Day* and *House Beautiful*. Magazine and newspaper experience gave her the very background for public relations that she would later require in those who sought to work with her.

Since its inception in 1938, Miss Ducas has served the National Foundation for Infantile Paralysis, starting out on a part-time basis, for the most part in a journalistic capacity. During the war, for two years, she served in Washington as chief of the Magazine Bureau of the Office of War Information, handling public relations with the national magazines and supplying them with information. Resuming her work for the Foundation in 1944, she was appointed director of public relations in 1949. To appreciate fully the capacity for accomplishment of this remarkably energetic woman, you should know that in private life she is Mrs. James B. Herzog, wife of a foreign trade executive and mother of two grown sons. Think of Miss Ducas the next time you complain of a heavy schedule!

Were you to look in on her busy department which is housed in downtown Manhattan's Equitable Building, you would find more than two dozen people in addition to the eight public relations men who serve in the field. "We insist on newspaper experience or its equivalent on a news magazine or the news side of radio, as a prerequisite for employment," Miss Ducas told us. "The reason for this is that our major ways of reaching the public are through the newspapers, magazines, radio, and TV, so we must know what the editor or program director expects to find in our material. This policy was very helpful to us when we handled the public relations and public information programs for the Polio Vaccine Trials, an event which was one of the big news stories from April through June of 1954, and which presented a wide variety of public relations problems."

The complete public acceptance of the Polio Vaccine Trials and the enthusiastic public endorsement of the Foundation, as evidenced by the public's increased support of the annual fund raising drives, are a tribute to the kind of public relations job Miss Ducas and her staff have done for the Foundation.

The public relations department of a national health agency like Miss Ducas' organization is responsible for the following activities:

Publishing and distributing information materials for the general public.

Publishing a monthly house organ, "The National Foundation News," for volunteers and staff.

Preparing and distributing the organization's annual report.

Providing speech material and publicity guides for volunteers.

Producing booklets, leaflets, newspaper releases, magazine articles.

Answering much of the correspondence that is received at national headquarters.

Obtaining and distributing photographs and art materials.

In addition to the above duties, Miss Ducas' department is responsible for making all arrangements for the nationwide tour of the Poster Child who is selected each year before the annual March of Dimes starts.

The number of health agencies in this country is continually growing, although few approach the size of the National Foundation for Infantile Paralysis. Nevertheless, large or small, they all have the same basic public relations problems—informing the public about their activities. New opportunities for men and women are continually opening up in this field, which is dedicated to the purpose of making life worth living.

Because of its size and nationwide organization, the National Foundation can afford and justify such a large public relations department. Agencies with smaller budgets must be content with smaller staffs but their need for good public relations and publicity people is no less acute.

2. *HOSPITALS*

Every year approximately one out of seven Americans enters a hospital. The fifth largest industry in the United States is accounted for by the 7,000-odd hospitals which employ more than two and a half million people (including students and volunteers). These institutions are providing more job opportunities for a growing number of public relations people who are serving hospitals and also medical societies. Our hospital needs continue to expand as more and more families are covered by medical, accident, health, and hospitalization insurance, as the life span increases, and as our population grows. This opens up opportunities for those interested in applying public relations to the general field of medicine by interpreting the work and accomplishments of a large hospital and the medical profession.

3. *WELFARE AGENCIES*

You are probably familiar with your town's annual community chest, United Fund, or Red Feather drive for funds to support the local charitable agencies. Where a community chest is established there is but one appeal for funds to support all the various participating health and welfare agencies. In large cities a community chest becomes big business and there is continual need for a good public relations program that will arouse and keep up public interest and acceptance of the chest.

Large charitable agencies like the famous Salvation Army often employ public relations or publicity staffs in major cities. There is a close correlation between fund raising and developing a good public relations program so that the two jobs often go hand in hand, and fund raising is a logical part of the duties of the public relations or publicity department.

4. *YOUTH ORGANIZATIONS*

Mary J. Shelly, director of public relations for the Girl Scouts of the United States of America, has a job that covers the nation and deals with the wave of the future—young girls between the ages of eight and sixteen. Today the Girl Scouts are 1,500,000 strong and in the next ten years it is predicted that the organization could grow to much greater size.

For a nationwide organization such as the Girl Scouts, Miss Shelly's familiarity with various sections of the country should prove extremely helpful. Born in the Middle West, she received her A.B. from the University of Oregon and her M.A. from Columbia University. She has spent a large part of her life interpreting to the public experiments in education and other fields. Perhaps Miss Shelly is best known for her direction of the Bennington College summer school devoted to the fine arts, and for clarifying to the public the new program of education for women which the college instituted in 1932.

During World War II, Miss Shelly served in the Women's Reserve of the Navy on Mildred McAfee Horton's immediate staff, giving direction to the training program for more than 125,000 women. After the war, she returned to Bennington and stayed until 1951 when the Secretary and the Chief of Staff of the Air Force asked her to reorganize the peacetime program for women in that service. A major part of this important assignment was the development of public understanding and acceptance of the military profession for women. Again Vermont claimed Miss Shelly but when Miss Stratton sent her challenging offer in 1954, Miss Shelly resigned as assistant to the president of Bennington College and joined the Girl Scouts.

By any standards the Girl Scout movement is large—a million and and a half children under the direction of a half million adult leaders, more than 39 per cent of whom are volunteer workers. Part of the organization's success is due to the fact that it places responsibility for doing the job directly on the leaders of the 1,400 local councils which sponsor some two thousand troops. Each council is autonomous but operates under the policies and guidance issued from the national office. The councils elect delegates to the National Council which, in turn, elects a board of directors to act as the top policy-making and governing body. The bulk of the responsibility for planning and guiding the over-all work of the organization falls on the national executive director and her staff.

The national organization, with headquarters in New York City, supervises the training of personnel, guides and helps local councils and troops, and publishes innumerable handbooks and other material for the leaders and their Scouts. In the national headquarters office there are about two hundred executives who provide the widely scattered councils with the materials, directions, and inspiration they need to do an effective job. Obviously public relations stands high on the list as one of the very important functions of the headquarters office.

The public relations staff under Miss Shelly's direction is essentially an interpretive service for Scouts and the public. The Public Information Division prepares and issues all releases to the newspapers, radio, and TV, answers inquiries and correspondence from the public, writes the Annual Report to Congress (the organization received its charter from the United States Congress in 1950 and must therefore make a yearly report on its activities), and prepares the annual Pictorial Review. Miss Shelly calls this review the Girl Scout "calling card" because it is used widely for such purposes as fund raising to typify the essence of the Girl Scout program. In addition, the public information staff provides the local councils with information that will assist them in doing a good public relations job.

The Publications Division functions somewhat like a publishing house. Whenever a department plans to issue a new publication, its "experts" prepare the text and in consultation with the Publications Division, agree on the best method of presenting and distributing it. The Publications Division then edits the material and takes full responsibility for processing and promoting it.

"Audio-visual aids, handled by the section of that name, provide one of the best means of getting our story across," Miss Shelly said. "So far we have only scratched the surface but we shall place a great deal more emphasis on them in the future. We have, of course, already produced many films, film strips and audio-visual aids for both national and local use."

The day we met Miss Shelly she had previewed a Senior

Girl Scout picture, "Mariners Ahoy," which was produced by the Girl Scouts in cooperation with Warner Brothers. "Another film is in production," she told us. "It centers about Scouting projects in Finland, Greece, Burma and the United States. We hope that this picture will interest people in Scouting and also excite them about our international friendship program."

The Community Relations Division is responsible for promoting closer relations with other organizations whose aims and ideals are similar to those of the Girl Scouts. This is done by close affiliation with many such groups and by providing local leaders with helpful information. Liaison with the World Association of Girl Guides and Girl Scouts is maintained by the International Division.

One special promotion on which Miss Shelly's department commenced work in 1954 is the Senior Round-Up to be held during the summer of 1956 in the Highland Recreation Area of Michigan. "Americana" is to be the theme and about 4,000 Senior Scouts are expected to come from every part of the nation. Each group attending is planning its program well in advance. It is hoped that this gathering will not only give the participants a new understanding of the significance of the Scouting movement but also a better appreciation of America and its heritage.

"It is absolutely essential to us that the public understand and believe in Girl Scouting because our program lives at the grass roots—in each community which provides both the leadership and the funds to support the local troop," Miss Shelly explained. "Women who assist the Scouting movement give generously of their time and they must not only believe in the importance of what they are doing but be respected by the community if they are going to do a good job. The national organization gives the program to the field and helps put it in action. Basically ours is a very simple concept: 'On my honor I will try to do my duty to God and my country.' That is all there is to it. Our public relations program is aimed at keeping the Scouting name and aim before the public as well as to tell about our good deeds!"

Are you interested in serving a youth organization such as the Girl Scouts, the Boy Scouts, Camp Fire Girls, a local Y.M.C.A., Y.W.C.A., Y.M.H.A. or a similar group, many of which have public relations departments? If so, Miss Shelly said, you must like young people, enjoy working with them and have a sincere desire to participate in youth character-building activities. Experience as a trooper or as a counselor in a summer camp or with a Scouting or other youth organization is extremely valuable. A well-rounded background, a knowledge of the contemporary scene—young people live now, not yesterday—a sense of financial responsibility because you must constantly think of your budget, an ability to do public speaking and to write, familiarity with how the press works—all these are important qualifications.

5. *LIBRARIES*

Were you to pass by the famous lions that guard the mammoth New York Public Library and drop in on the relaxed and charming young woman who is one of the library's top administrative officers, you would never suspect that she shoulders the entire responsibility for the system's complex public relations program. Public relations is a profession to which Anna Glantz just naturally gravitated, and as director of public relations for the New York Public Library she has her fingers on the pulse of one of the largest library systems in the world.

A graduate of Goucher, Miss Glantz worked in the college library following graduation and became head of the circulation department. During her spare time she wrote for professional periodicals and developed a skill that soon proved very useful—as anyone in public relations will tell you. From Goucher she went directly to the New York Public Library as assistant to the chief of circulation. Here she became interested in the library's budget problem since at that time —in 1944—the library was receiving but 48¢ per capita support from the city, next to the lowest large-city rate in the entire country. It seemed obvious to Miss Glantz that the Board of Estimate (which has a hand on the city purse strings) and the public would have to know about the library's financial struggles before increased support would be made available. Volunteering her services after hours, Miss Glantz helped tackle the problem and as a result of her efforts the press was called in to get the first complete and factual story of the library's financial plight. That year additional funds were voted for the library.

At about the same time, the library started an adult education program and it quickly became evident that it would be necessary to publicize this new undertaking if the vast public which the library serves was ever to learn about it. As a result of the successful publicity again created by Miss Glantz, the importance of public relations and its attendant promotion was recognized and a new department was organized with Miss Glantz at the head.

Since that time the department has steadily grown in size and importance until today it is responsible for the following activities:

1. Formulation and execution of over-all public relations program for the New York Public Library. This includes the main building and the eighty branches, numbered among which are the Municipal Reference Library and the Municipal Archives and Records Library.
2. Planning and handling all publicity for newspapers,

radio, and television for the main building and the eighty branches—a staggering undertaking by itself!

3. Staffing the inquiry desk in the main lobby—an important function since it is here that visitors get their first impression of the library.
4. Handling the sale of all library publications.
5. Preparation of the art work for use in promotions, special publications, and exhibitions.
6. Co-ordinating the publication of the many pamphlets and other material published by the library.
7. Teaching new employees the nature and value of public relations. This is done at semi-annual orientation meetings.

"The public library," Miss Glantz told us, "is an educational institution that has an obligation to extend education to the people of the country. We must let them know about the library, its activities, and facilities. We must do everything possible to invite them to use it."

Miss Glantz believes that this is achieved only if every staff member is public relations minded and there is constant promotion of all library activities that are taking place in the huge central building with its twenty-one divisions, as well as in the eighty branches. In order to co-ordinate effectively the public relations program, Miss Glantz explained that she relied to a large extent on the initiative of the branch librarians and division heads to suggest material and ideas for publicity and special promotions in their units, but that all the actual public relations activities are planned and carried out by her staff which operate from the main building.

Public relations has paid off handsomely to the library. You see it reflected in the courteous employees. You read about it continually in your newspaper. You cannot help but be impressed by the growing circulation figures and the municipal financial support the library receives each year despite the perpetual fiscal emergency that plagues City Hall. Yes, public relations under Anna Glantz's capable direction is as important to the library as its stacks of books!

Every librarian should understand the importance of public relations, for she deals continually with the public, and the library is often judged by the impression she makes on the patrons. Unfortunately, not every public library is large enough to afford a public relations director like Miss Glantz, but remember—you future librarians who may be bitten by the public relations bug—Miss Glantz was responsible for the creation of the public relations department in the New York Public Library. Go thou and do likewise!

Public libraries, by their very name and function, deal directly with the public, and good public relations is a must, for it is the source of the librarians' bread and butter. College and university libraries, on the other hand, have the primary responsibility of providing good library service only for their students and faculty members. Because this is a "captive audience," some college and university library administrators fail to recognize that there is, nevertheless, a need for a conscious public relations program.

Another type of library has developed to meet the needs of business and other organizations for specialized information. You will find that most large companies have one or more such libraries, usually referred to as *special libraries,* to provide for their executives and employees the information they need. Like the college library which serves a limited clientele and therefore normally does not have relationships with the public, the special library primarily serves the employees of its organization. Some of the more progressive special libraries have found that there is a public which looks to them for specialized library service. There are customers, competitors, government workers, researchers, students, and even the bona fide public. Business now recognizes that by catering to the needs of those outside the company, the special library can make a substantial contribution to the company's over-all public relations program.

Under the able leadership of Elizabeth Ferguson, librarian of the Institute of Life Insurance, the role of public relations in the special library is being increasingly publicized. Special Libraries Association sponsors frequent forums and meetings on the subject with the result that although no special library has its public relations director, librarians know the importance of public relations and are learning how to put its principles into everyday practice.

6. *RELIGIOUS ORGANIZATIONS*

If you have traveled on the Hudson Tubes in New York, the streetcars in Vancouver, or in the Chicago subways, you may have noticed a car card advertising an entirely different product. The same type of ad has appeared in mining camps near the Arctic Circle, on a large billboard near a New Jersey beach, and in approximately forty countries and in many languages. Copy for these ads is taken directly from the Bible since "Best Seller Publicity" sells nothing except trust in God and faith in Jesus Christ.

"Best Seller Publicity" has been "selling" faith to troubled people since 1937 when Miss Jo Peterson decided that millions of unhappy people would be helped by religion but no one had successfully reached them with its message. The idea of using car cards came to her as she rode to work on a crowded bus, and a short time later she secured the help of a dozen prominent women who agreed to form "Best Seller Publicity." The first text chosen was "Come unto me, all ye that labor and are heavy laden, and I will give you rest." This appeared in 250 Chicago streetcars and the response was immediate. Letters, inquiries, contributions, and offers of help flooded the tiny office and the project was off to a real start.

Since then the work of the organization has spread throughout the world and for the most part has concentrated its activities by displaying its message in streetcars and busses, on billboards, and by distributing small copies of the placards by hand.

"Best Seller Publicity" is a good example of a special type of evangelism which is a form of religious publicity. An evangelist is a teller of the "good news," which to Christians means telling about Jesus Christ. In theory every Christian should be a publicist for his religion; however, in practice, most professed believers leave it up to the ministers and other trained or paid workers to tell the "good news." Among other faiths there are many sects that are just as anxious to spread the news about their beliefs. However, in this country they are for the most part small groups and therefore cannot afford to spend as much on propagation of their faith as the various Christian denominations.

If you have strong religious convictions and a deep-rooted desire to serve your church in some public relations capacity, you should know that little monetary reward awaits you. A very modest salary is the best that most church organizations can afford to pay, but people who enter this type of service are dedicated to a cause that seeks no personal gain. Unless you are dedicated to your religion and anxious to give unselfishly of your time and labor, we strongly urge you to practice public relations elsewhere.

Today, the more progressive sects utilize all the modern techniques of communications to teach the young, train and inspire their leaders, raise money, carry their message, and keep their members informed of the activities of the church. There are more than a hundred Protestant journals and innumerable magazines published for the Catholic laity that reach millions of people. Many of these periodicals offer opportunities for writers, reporters, and other interested workers.

For the most part those who are engaged in directing the publicity or public relations work for church organizations are either men who have prepared for the ministry or are trained leaders. Should you be interested in doing public relations for your church, we suggest you discuss the matter with your pastor and/or write to the national headquarters office of your church. Explain your interest in public relations, ask what opportunities exist in the church and if any special training is required. Certainly any young person who is drawn to the general field of public relations can find an interesting and inspiring niche in his or her church organization and make a valuable contribution to the faith.

Women do not necessarily monopolize social and religious agencies as you might be led to believe because all of the personalities introduced in this chapter happened to be of that sex. However, we should point out that salaries paid by organizations that for the most part depend on voluntary contributions for their support are usually modest and therefore generally attract more women than men. There are exceptions, however, and the entire field is wide open to both men and women. There are positions that command good salaries and these are by no means monopolized by the men.

CHAPTER

10

How Public Relations Serves Education

A TEEN-AGER once asked his father what business he would recommend for a career. The young man was seeking something that would not be affected by a major depression or made obsolete by technological advances.

"My son," the father replied, "people will always eat, so there will be a constant need for producers and sellers of food. People will always die, so the undertaking business will never become obsolete. One further thing of which you can be sure, women will always want to be glamorous, so the cosmetic business is a sure bet!"

What he failed to mention was the fact that children will always be going to school. Education is one of the nation's largest businesses and remains essential in war and peace, depression and prosperity.

As the cost of education continues to rise, educators are becoming increasingly aware of the need for better public understanding of the schools' problem. It is unrealistic to expect the schools to undertake an effective teaching program without being able to pay for it. Building, salary, and operating costs have all increased drastically since 1945 and most communities have experienced a substantial population growth which creates need for additional schools. Acquainting the public with its aims, plans, program, and problems is a necessary activity of every school if it hopes to win the confidence and support of the community.

The School's Publics

Every school is constantly being observed and judged by several groups of people, each eyeing its activities from a different point of view. Keeping every group satisfied is a difficult if not impossible job, particularly in the case of a large school system or university. As we shall see below, the students are not the school's only "publics." It must cater to the whims and wishes of others as well. These people include:

Parents of Students

Quick to pick up and magnify complaints of their children, parents are often critical of many phases of the school program.

Faculty Members

Teachers and college professors have never been overpaid. Today, many public school teachers are forced to work longer hours where the school and teacher shortage necessitates split sessions. Keeping the loyalty, interest, and enthusiasm of the teacher is a must in every school if there is to be an effective teaching program.

School Board or Trustees

This small but important group of individuals is responsible for the over-all direction of a school or college and approves all appointments. It must be thoroughly satisfied with the job performance of the faculty and those connected with the school.

Taxpayers

The taxpayer's lot is never a happy one and were it not for the school tax, his bank account would be quite a bit larger. School boards seldom find him enthusiastic over proposals to spend money—particularly if he is along in years and has no children! Too often he doesn't properly understand why the school needs more income from the school district.

Alumni

Not only do loyal alumni of privately supported institutions provide many freshmen for their alma mater by sending their children and recommending the college to their friends, but they are becoming an important source for funds. Keeping the enthusiasm and backing of this group is essential to the well-being of any institution.

The Public

Every school, college and university wants to be well thought of by the general public; otherwise it may be difficult to find new students or extra money to operate.

State Legislature

State-supported colleges and universities must earn the legislature's support, for it is that body which holds the major purse strings.

There are few institutions that have as many "publics" to consider as the school, college, or university. The following list highlights the problem of each type of school:

Type of School	*Publics to be considered*
Public School	Taxpayers
	Parents
	Local Residents
	Board of Education
	Faculty
	Students

Type of School	*Publics to be considered*
Private School	General public
Endowed College	Local residents
Endowed University	Alumni Trustees Parents and prospective parents Students and prospective students
Tax-supported college or university	Same as above list plus: State legislature

1. *PUBLIC SCHOOLS*

The idea of establishing public relations programs for tax-supported secondary schools is gradually becoming more prevalent as thoughtful community leaders realize that it is essential to win public and taxpayer support for the local school program. After you read about the public relations programs in Cincinnati and Wilmington, you will better understand how public relations serves the public schools.

A Pioneer in His Field

In 1935 a survey of the Cincinnati Public Schools was made by a staff of educators who decided they were suffering from a lack of publicity and that the school, public, and community relations were of the "hit and miss" order. Two years later the Cincinnati Board of Education organized a Department of Community Relations and selected John F. Locke as its director.

Mr. Locke, now serving his second term as president of the National School Public Relations Association, is a soft-spoken veteran of World War I who comes from "Down East." He taught in Cincinnati vocational schools for sixteen years prior to his appointment. Before he had been in his new assignment many weeks, the editors and reporters were unanimous in stating that he was doing exactly the kind of a job the survey indicated was needed. Now when a city editor, or anyone else for that matter, wants a story or information about one or more of Cincinnati's 90 schools, he calls up John Locke.

Statistical evidence of Mr. Locke's success in the field of community relations was quickly shown by the city elections. The year he was appointed as director of Community Relations, the operational levy (or tax) for the schools received only a 50.7 per cent vote. In 1939 it went to 52.8 per cent and shot up to 66.8 per cent in 1942. Average vote in seven extra-levy campaigns since 1937 was 60 per cent. Four bond issue campaigns totaling fifty-seven and a half million dollars for new school buildings have been approved by the voters by per cents ranging from 64 to 83.

Mr. Locke's three-fold function is (1) to picture to Cincinnati people the things their schools are trying to do, how they are trying to do them, and how well they are succeeding, (2) to administer a program for enabling the public to use its school buildings, and (3) to promote among the staff of each school a better understanding of the problems and policies of the school system.

"What more than 30,000,000 children in our nation's almost 300,000 schools, taught by over 1,000,000 teachers, do and how they do it is news," Mr. Locke said. "When I help the press get news stories or supply prepared material, I have three yardsticks by which I measure every release: It must be news, it must be truthful, and it must be factual."

Mr. Locke believes that public opinion always has and always will direct the course of events in America but that our schools cannot afford to keep quiet about their contribution to the responsibility for the future peace and prosperity of the world. The schools may be doing the best job in the world but if it is done behind closed doors and the world doesn't know about it, it does not constitute a good job. It is necessary that we make possible a continuation of the good work and that involves helping the press to get news.

"I feel it is important to distinguish between publicity and news. I believe publicity is something you want the reader to read, news is something the reader wants to read. Newspapers consider it their function to tell the facts and the philosophy behind the facts so their readers can find their way. It is true that newspapers support causes and they can exert influence in a direct and indirect manner but with courage, vision, intelligence, independence and integrity, they report and interpret news and information for the public."

Wilmington Has an Effective Program

"I am not sure that ours is a typical public relations program in education," says John L. Hunt, Co-ordinator of School-Community Relations for the city of Wilmington, Delaware, "but we arrived at it through the process of trial and error and it seems to work. No one technique for operating a school public relations program would be applicable to all schools. Any program must be based on a thorough knowledge of the community and must work within the framework of the existing organization."

The city of Wilmington, which contains about half the population of Delaware, is perhaps best known as the home of E. I. DuPont de Nemours & Company as well as the corporate home office of thousands of companies which are incorporated in Delaware. By 1955 the city's population exceeded 125,000 and its public school system with its staff of 700 was educating some 14,000 children in its 21 schools.

"School-community relations in Wilmington is a two-way process," Mr. Hunt explained. "First, there is interpretation of the schools for the public by every available means of communication. Secondly, there is participation by laymen in the planning and policy making of the school program."

Mr. Hunt considers the most insignificant announcement about a school meeting or activity as important a part of the total program of interpretation as the editorialized type of material which attempts to explain why schools operate as they do. No one avenue of communication is better than another, the variety of publics must be reached through a variety of media.

Briefly, here are the means of communication Mr. Hunt uses to reach the public:

Press

Every school has its own teacher-reporter. Principals, department heads, and other members of the administrative staff are urged to release to the papers all newsworthy stories. These need not be pre-cleared with Mr. Hunt's office. A continuous flow of news items regarding the schools comes across his desk daily and when he sees a story possibility he immediately puts reporters on its trail. Mr. Hunt's complete clipping file of all school stories averages 1,000 news releases per school year in the local press. This number is exclusive of sports stories.

Radio

Each morning from Tuesday through Friday the largest local radio station, WDEL, broadcasts school news using high school seniors as announcers. Saturday mornings Mr. Hunt presents a fifteen-minute program, "Learning to Live," a documentary tape recording made during the week in various schools. These recordings include musical programs, dramatics, special assemblies, and interviews with all types of groups as well as individuals in classrooms, gymnasiums, locker rooms, corridors and other places.

Television

Each Sunday afternoon a half-hour program entitled "School Report," similar to the radio program, "Learning to Live," is organized and produced by Mr. Hunt. The Department of Child Development and Guidance also conducts a series of telecasts that give high school seniors an opportunity to interview representatives of business, industry, and the professions as to vocational opportunities.

School Publications

"Our Schools," a monthly publication, seeks to interpret various phases of the school program and is mailed to about 7,500 citizens including Parent-Teacher Association members, parents of kindergarten children and representative business and professional people.

Speakers Bureau

More than 60 members of the school staff have consented to speak on different aspects of the educational program when a speaker is requested by an organization in the community.

The community participates too through formal P.T.A.'s, homeroom groups and Mother's Clubs. A body known as the Home and School Council, made up of representatives from each parent group, considers matters of policy and program in the over-all system. A Vocational Guidance Committee, made up of representatives from a number of city business and industrial groups, is called together frequently to plan career guidance television programs, career days in the schools, and other activities designed to help young people choose the proper vocation. Twenty craft committees, made up of employers and representatives of labor, advise the teachers and administration of the vocational school.

Citizens groups have been formed from time to time when special problems arise. In 1947 lay representatives served on a thorough self-survey of all school departments. Citizens served on committees appointed to study the needs of the community for new schools and how best to meet them. One such committee was appointed by the Superintendent of Schools to make a study of salaries and employment practices in the city. Two other committees composed of doctors and dentists give medical and dental counsel to the school system.

Practically every school building which has auditorium or gymnasium facilities is open every night of the week for use by organized groups in the community. The schools co-operate and work closely with all community groups, such as churches, service clubs, Y.M. and Y.W.C.A.'s, Scouts, and others.

"The Wilmington system claims no originality or special excellence," Mr. Hunt told us. "As far as we can tell, public education has a very healthy backing throughout the city. However, we are not complacent and realize that something may break out at any time. Therefore, the best preventive for this we feel is a continuous interrelation of the school and the community."

In reply to our question: "How did you get into public relations?" Mr. Hunt answered:

"I, like many other public relations people in the educational field, entered the profession through the door of education because of personality characteristics that seemed to adapt me for this type of work.

"My advice to young people who would prepare for this type of work is to go in strongly for extracurricular activities, work in organizations, help put out the school paper and yearbook, take part in plays to gain stage confidence, go to conferences, and meet people. There are classroom teachers who might not agree with this advice but I am personally convinced that participation in this type of activity in high school and college days did more to prepare me for this type of profession than any formal classroom work."

2. *PRIVATE SCHOOLS*

Undoubtedly the schools most in need of a good public relations program are the private or "prep" schools. As many of them grew they naturally attracted children of wealthy families. "Snob appeal" is what many have often been accused of practicing and this stigma is something they are trying to overcome. Today most private schools seek their students from families of every income group because this gives them a more democratic and better balanced group of students.

"A Nose for News"

At a time when stories of hydrogen bombs, new world tensions, war, hurricanes, and political scandals fill our newspapers and national magazines, it would hardly seem possible that the dedication of a lantern by the Japanese ambassador at a small Connecticut school would hold any interest for the nation's press. But Bernard Hammons' nose started to twitch and tingle the minute he learned that His Excellency, Mr. Sadao Iguchi, Ambassador of Japan to the United States, would dedicate an Ishidoro (a Japanese stone lantern) at his school during Parents' Week End. His carefully prepared press releases with their distinctive and eye-catching band of red and blue, gave the metropolitan reporters all the advance information they would need to write a good story. And because they knew Bernie Hammons and his reputation for sending releases only when he had a real story to tell, the response—which included a request from *Life* for pictures to do a possible cover story—was immediate! What might well have passed as a very insignificant affair received amazing coverage in the nation's press, thanks to a well thought out and continuing public relations program.

The day after we wrote Bernard Hammons of Avon Old Farms School for some information about his public relations activities, we received a long distance phone call. "You've simply got to come up and see Avon Old Farms for yourself, it's a terrific story!" It didn't require much imagination to realize that there must be an unusual story at Mr. Hammons' end of the wire and as you will see, there was! Not only is his story unusual but it is an excellent example of public relations at work in a brand-new field. As the result of Mr. Hammons' recent activities, other private schools are now recognizing the importance of public relations and following suit.

Situated near Hartford, Connecticut, on more than three thousand acres of rolling wood and farm land, Avon Old Farms School is a fascinating bit of the old world transplanted to the new. The buildings, made of native reddish stone, have irregular slate roofs which dip steeply over the leaded windows. Norman archways tunnel through solid masonry to give a suggestion of a village in the English Cotswolds.

The school was designed and built in the 1920's by the late Mrs. Theodate Pope Riddle of nearby Farmington as a memorial to her father. Not only was Mrs. Riddle an architect of note but she had many forward-looking ideas about education. Fearing that educational techniques were becoming too standardized, she was determined that there should be no typically molded Avonian and she founded the school on the basic concept that "the ways in which people differ are more important than the ways in which they are alike."

Bernard Hammons, our tall, good-looking and warm host

at Avon Old Farms School, is the kind of man whom at the first hand shake, you feel you've always known. He loves his work. He lives it and talks about it constantly, but wouldn't you too, if you wore as many hats as he? His official title is assistant to the provost but he is also director of public relations, admissions officer, secretary of the Alumni Association, director of fund raising, faculty advisor for the school paper and yearbook, and, we suspect, a lot more. "Everything I do concerns human relations, which, after all, is only one phase of public relations," Mr. Hammons observed.

"Bernie" Hammons, as he is known throughout Connecticut, is a good example of a public relations man who had no formal training. "I've always had a natural nose for news," he admits and his bulging scrapbook containing press clippings about the school and his own varied activities are ample proof that he puts his nose to good use. As a boy he was fascinated by printing and spent his afternoons and Saturdays working in the local print shop. A devotee of polo, he played polo in the National Guard, worked his school team to within one point of the national championship, and did promotional work on the side to insure a good audience for his winning team. A successful salesman and real estate broker, he returned in 1947 at the request of Donald W. Pierpont, provost, to serve as advisor to Mr. Pierpont in the reorganization and development program of the school.

"My public relations reponsibilities are a natural outgrowth of my other duties," he explained as we walked through the cheerful quadrangle that echoed with the laughter of boys preparing for the big football game with Kingswood. "Hi, George," Mr. Hammons called to a tall redhead. "A filet mignon for every touchdown you make!" He meant it too but confided that he feared there would be no payoff necessary.

"Actually our school was faced with a most trying situation

in 1948," he said. "It reopened after being used during the war by the army as a rehabilitation center for the blind. We had no alumni organization, no recognition in the academic world or the community, and our public was—well, frankly—skeptical and hostile, for we were classed as a 'snob' school but one without proper ancestors. We acknowledged the problem and decided that the best way to solve it was to develop consciously a 'Service to Community' program." As two boys approached, Mr. Hammons greeted each by name and asked if they were going to the game. "Oh yes, sir," they answered almost simultaneously. You could tell by their happy grins what they thought of Mr. Hammons.

We stood looking out over the expanse of autumn-colored hills and he continued: "Under our community program we offered the use of our buildings, our three-thousand-acre estate, and all our facilities to groups in neighboring communities as well as to other schools, colleges, and organizations."

To win acceptance in the local community, here are just a few of the activities to which the school invites the public during the school year: Sunday afternoon concerts, lectures, free evening adult-education programs, special music events, annual hunter trials and other outdoor events for the benefit of local charities. The program is succeeding too! One villager sent a check because he liked the services the school was rendering the community even though he didn't have time to use them.

It was also recognized that the alumni who were scattered far and wide must be found and interested in the rebirth of their alma mater. By forming an alumni organization, holding frequent meetings at school for grads, sending them copies of the school paper and other material of interest about the school, a loyal and enthusiastic alumni body has been created. The former graduates now regularly contribute to the alumni fund, serve on endowment committees, act on New Boy committees and officiate on the board of directors.

During the first five years that he served as director of public relations, Mr. Hammons estimates that his program brought 45,000 people to the school campus. He has maintained a consistent information program of news releases, Sunday supplement stories and magazine articles; 380 news releases, or 98 per cent of those submitted during one year, appeared in the press throughout the country. He has originated over 30 radio and TV shows and in his spare time he handles special publicity for public events ranging in nature from Carnegie Hall concerts to model plane meets, horse events, educational and religious conferences. From time to time he serves as a public relations consultant for large corporations.

Perhaps the most impressive thing about Mr. Hammons is not the tremendous amount of favorable mention he garners for the school from all over the nation, but rather his dislike of publicity as such and the sincerity of his belief that public relations earns good will only through good deeds. "Are you willing to do a good deed?" he asks. If so, the good deeds will generate your publicity. "Everything you do comes back a thousand times," he insists.

Another of Mr. Hammons' convictions is that a good public relations man is never satisfied unless he's done his very best—"gone beyond the call of duty," as he puts it. And to illustrate what he means he told of a request he received one afternoon from a New York TV station for some moving-picture film to be used on an educational program.

"When do you want it?" he asked and the caller told him that the following Tuesday would do. "You'll have it tomorrow morning," Mr. Hammons said. Most of that night was spent editing and splicing film and he was aboard the first plane out of Hartford the next morning. The film was duly delivered to the TV producer and as Mr. Hammons was about to leave, someone reminded the producer that he still hadn't obtained a headmaster to appear on the program.

"I've got your headmaster," Mr. Hammons almost shouted. "Donald Pierpont will be glad to appear on your program." That Sunday millions of people had their first introduction to Avon Old Farms School and met its provost because its public relations director believes in doing a thorough job.

It would require an enormous book to chronicle the many activities of this remarkable man. Always giving of his time and energy to help others, he is constantly being called upon to assist here and there. He has a nose for news but also a heart that is quick to respond when anyone is in trouble. Under his philosophy Avon Old Farms School has earned the deep respect of its neighbors and alumni, the press, and an ever growing number of men and women who live all the way from Maine to California.

3. *COLLEGES AND UNIVERSITIES*

Institutions of higher education are becoming more and more aware of the need for telling others about themselves and their good deeds. We have already noted how many publics they must impress favorably, now let's see how the job is done by a college, and then by a university.

"It's a Small College"

"It is, sir, as I have said, a small college, and yet there are those that love it. . . ." Daniel Webster told the Supreme Court in 1818 when he pleaded the famous Dartmouth College case. Today, almost 200 years after its founding, that statement is still true, for by comparision with many universities, Dartmouth's enrollment of less than 3,000 students classes her as a small college. And there are those who love her, particularly some 27,000 alumni, most of whom are extremely loyal and vocal public relations representatives for their alma mater.

In January of 1952, President Dickey appointed a committee to study the objectives of the college's public relations program. It was asked to define them, to measure them against what was actually being done, and to advise what further steps should be taken. The committee recognized that by and large Dartmouth's public relations were good, probably better than those of many colleges but susceptible of improvement. The college had grown, it had become big business, and there was some doubt that its public relations had kept pace with its growth.

At its first meeting the committee, led by its distinguished alumnus, Francis Brown, editor of the New York *Times Book Review*, agreed that Dartmouth's public relations program should be guided by the principle that Dartmouth is an educational institution. Obvious though that finding seems, its enunciation by an independent committee provided a guiding principle which has become the cornerstone and yardstick for the entire public relations program. According to Mr. Brown, the basic purpose of Dartmouth's public relations program is "to tell and explain to all concerned or even mildly interested what the college is up to and why. In other words, those conducting the college's public relations activities are themselves involved in education, in spreading knowledge that ultimately could be the foundation for sound opinions about Dartmouth today."

Feeling that perhaps the college had established a reputation more for its Winter Carnival and jovial houseparty week ends than as an educational institution, the committee decided that the time was ripe to show the college in its proper perspective.

Just as we found there are several publics a college must reach, so are there many tools with which to do the job. Some of these used at Dartmouth—in addition to the usual straight news releases and the monthly Alumni Magazine—are periodic bulletins aimed at secondary school teachers, a special magazine for non-alumni parents, reprints of pertinent speeches of the president and articles from the *Alumni Magazine,* the Dartmouth calendar, and numerous pamphlets and other publications, each devoted to a different aspect of the college and its educational program. In the audio-visual field there are film slides, recordings, and movies like "My First Week at Dartmouth," also films for TV.

Officers and faculty members of the college make many visits to secondary schools, speak to far-flung alumni groups, address conferences of educators, and write books and articles for publication. Each year thousands of people visit Dartmouth. They include tourists, special convention groups, alumni and their families, parents of students and prospective students, educators, distinguished visitors and speakers, and—of course—attractive representatives of many women's colleges. The department of public relations helps to see that everything possible is done to make visitors feel welcome and at home while staying in Hanover.

College sports stories, whether there be victory or defeat, are not difficult to place but news about education is particularly lacking in interest for the average reader. It is not easy to shape an interesting story that deals with education or, if one is so written, to place it! The committee recognized the need for obtaining a man who not only had a good nose for educational news but an ability to write and place such items. The man finally chosen for the job is a graduate of Harvard with a good background of journalism which he obtained at the *Providence Journal.*

Today the staff of the public relations department includes its executive head who is also secretary of the college, the assistant secretary of the college who is in charge of movies,

people, Mrs. Collier, as director of publicity, is official spokesman for the university and handles all of its publicity except that concerning sports, which now has its own publicity man. (She started this part of the university-wide program with a part-time assistant on sports.) In addition to her staff she has the help of the university's photo service and four student assistants from the School of Public Relations and Communications. Because the university is so large and spread out over a wide area geographically, each college has a student correspondent who is the bureau's contact for students and activities in his particular area. Mrs. Collier likes to experiment with new ideas and techniques. This was one of her experiments that has proven very successful and popular with the student body.

One member of the staff spends all his time preparing national-level copy, searching constantly for news that will command the attention of the wire services and important magazines. Here are examples of the kind of stories he has handled.

A faculty member gave a paper on the blasting of the earth's surface at a meeting of scientists in California. As soon as a news story covering his activitiy was released by the publicity bureau in Boston, it was picked up by many newspapers as well as *Time*, which did a story on it.

A special chorus and orchestra composed of Boston University students rehearsed for six weeks under Leopold Stokowski to give concerts in Boston and New York. This story was good for both local and national news and was well covered by the music press, local and national.

The College of Industrial Technology had been a strictly all-male proposition since its beginning in 1951 until a girl from Pittsfield, Massachusetts, was enrolled in 1954 to become the only girl among three hundred and eighty boys. That looked like a news story to Mrs. Collier—and indeed it was! It went out over the New England wire service, appeared in local papers, Pittsfield papers, and also in several scientific magazines.

"There's more news around our campus than our limited staff can hope to handle and we have to be very selective," Mrs. Collier said. "Basically we want to establish good public relations with sound principles behind them. To achieve this, we try to present the university to the public so it will know and understand our problems and objectives. I also feel that it is a responsibility of my agency to get a proper understanding of higher education in general."

Here is what Mrs. Collier has to say for young people thinking of entering the public relations field. "Nothing takes the place of a good liberal arts course plus graduate study in public relations, if a person can afford the time and money. Someone anxious to make a career in college or university public relations should start, after getting his formal education, by seeking a position as a staff assistant in a college public relations or publicity department.

"The applicant should be of excellent health with stamina to stand the intermittent pressures caused by unexpected emergencies, and should be the type of individual who is interested in building a future for his profession as well as doing a good productive job. Financial remuneration is better than it used to be, but people who wish to join the top income brackets had better look elsewhere for their life work."

American College Public Relations Association

During her early days with the publicity bureau, Mrs. Collier was shocked and discouraged by the way press relations were handled in many colleges. No wonder the colleges were receiving such shabby treatment by the newspapers! She thereupon joined the American College Public

Relations Association and helped pioneer the promotion of better professional standards for handling college and university publicity. As a past president of this organization, she has worked hard to move it towards its objectives.

Today the association tries to achieve its purpose by working with the public relations personnel and presidents of colleges and universities, helping them to keep abreast of and improve their public relations program, and on the national level, by working with other educational associations. Marvin Topping, executive secretary of the association, was trained for the ministry, having obtained his theological degree from Boston University School of Theology. His chief interest and concern has always been to work in education and he says that his greatest strength in the ministry was to work in developing the educational program of the church and youth organizations. No wonder that when an opportunity came to serve a church-related college as its public relations director, he accepted and has remained in public relations since that time.

IN CONCLUSION

We'll be surprised if this chapter hasn't been an eye-opener for you. Aside from the general field of business, education probably offers the greatest opportunity for you future public relations men and women. A rising birth rate, a growing insistence on making higher education available to more and more young people, and assured financial support by taxpayers and endowment funds makes education a field with unlimited horizons for those interested in practicing public relations.

CHAPTER

11

How Public Relations Serves Entertainment

There is no doubt that television has nosed ahead of aviation as the nation's number one glamour industry. Growing by leaps and bounds, attracting top artists and performers, jumping in no time at all from black and white to color, and becoming the standard topic of dinner conversation, television is undeniably part and parcel of the American way of life. Let's look in on giant NBC, the network that has 388 radio and television stations and whose television programs are seen by more people than those of any other network.

If you know something about the organization of broadcasting and television networks, you may better appreciate how publicity serves them. The National Broadcasting Company owns and operates five television and five radio stations (the maximum permitted by law), and these are located in New York, Washington, Chicago, Cleveland, Los Angeles (television only), and San Francisco (radio only). In addition to providing programs for its own stations, the network sends them by leased wire or microwave relay to stations scattered throughout the country. These independently owned stations may be affiliated with NBC and use their programs exclusively or they may contract for programs from NBC and use their programs exclusively or they may contract for programs from NBC and other networks. The program sponsor who foots the bill naturally is anxious to obtain the maximum coverage for his show (whether it be radio or television), and therefore the networks vie with each other to offer the greatest audiences. The more money a sponsor agrees to spend, the greater the number of network stations that can be included. You can see how important publicity is. Good publicity that pulls a large audience spells profits for the company because it means more advertising revenue from the sponsors.

To the vice-president of public relations report the following departments: Advertising and Promotion, Continuity Acceptance, Research and Press. It is with the latter that we are concerned in this chapter. Reporting to the vice-president of press are: the director of the press department, the manager of program publicity, the manager of business publicity, and the director of information. The business publicity manager furnishes news stories and information about NBC to the trade press. The director of information supervises the answering of audience mail, as well as inquiries from the public, and prepares speech material for company executives. As for program promotion—just read on.

We met Don Bishop of program publicity in his office on the third floor of the lofty RCA building which houses the main offices and the New York studios of the National Broadcasting Company. Mr. Bishop is a young and personable North Carolinian—without a southern accent! His office is just off the large press room where fifty-odd people devote all their efforts to telling the world about NBC, its many programs, and artists. Despite the noise of jiggling teletypes, jangling phones, staccato typewriters, and the rush of people scurrying about this busy office, you sense the purpose and well-planned organization behind all the activity.

"When I entered high school I knew that I wanted to get into newspaper work," Mr. Bishop told us. "I started writing for the local newspaper, *The New Bern Sun Journal,* and after graduation I purposely spent a year reporting sports and local news for the same paper before entering college."

At the University of North Carolina, Mr. Bishop naturally majored in journalism and *wrote.* Editing the college daily, preparing special articles on assignment, writing for the alumni magazine, and reporting student activities for the big *Winston-Salem Journal,* gave him the variety of writing experience he was seeking. During two summer vacations he worked on a local home town newspaper and earned the promise of a permanent job on the *Winston-Salem Journal,* as soon as he graduated. Unfortunately, Uncle Sam was waiting for him that June day in 1941 as he left commencement exercises and Private Bishop was soon in nearby Fort Bragg, taking basic training. Assigned to a specialist unit, he soon came to the notice of a public relations officer when some articles he wrote for the *Winston-Salem Journal* were submitted for approval. He was thereupon assigned to a replacement training center in the public relations office. After a year and a half of public relations, Sergeant Bishop decided that he was contributing too little to the war effort. He was accepted for Officer Candidate School, wound up as a motor officer, and then ironically enough, was assigned back to public relations.

It was during these war years that he developed an urge to teach journalism rather than be a reporter. Therefore when Lieutenant Bishop was discharged in December 1945, he took the job that still awaited him on the *Winston-Salem Journal* as a reporter—with the understanding that he would leave the following September to enter the Columbia University School of Journalism to get his M.S. and better qualify for a teaching position.

But something happened while he was at Columbia. Perhaps it was the proximity of Radio City which he frequently visited. Perhaps it was his contact with and growing awareness of the great future that lay ahead for television. At any rate, instead of contacting college presidents for a job, Mr. Bishop decided to try for a position in the press department at NBC. This wasn't easy, for competition was keen then as it is now, and he realized that he must do something to make himself stand apart from the other candidates. The break came when he noticed that Thor Johnson, who was leaving Juilliard School to conduct the Cincinnati Symphony Orchestra, bore a remarkable resemblance to the NBC artist, Kay Kyser, a fellow North Carolinian. Here was an excellent publicity possibility and he suggested that NBC take a picture of the "long hair" and "pop" musicians standing together. The picture, he pointed out, would be sure-fire promotion for NBC in Cincinnati and North Carolina as well. The idea was a good one because although the picture never materialized, Don Bishop got the job.

As one of the fifteen staff writers, each of whom is responsible for publicizing a certain number of shows or programs, Mr. Bishop was assigned educational, religious, and informational programs—the so-called "public service" programs. One of his first responsibilities was to handle the press publicity for the United Nations Week which observed the anniversary of the creation of the United Nations. When this special promotion ended, he learned of an opening for a specialist on the magazine staff which provides material about NBC for periodicals. From the position of magazine editor he was promoted to manager of program publicity in which position he expedites the assignments and co-ordinates all efforts of the staff writers and specialists. Working under

Mr. Bishop's direction are fifteen staff writers to whom are assigned the programs, nine photographers, two magazine specialists, three persons who specialize in providing news for the columnists, and several clerks. Although a staff writer has the responsibility for developing publicity for each of the programs assigned to him, he may call upon the photographers and magazine or columnist specialists to assist him.

"The primary job of the press department is to develop publicity for the NBC programs and personalities," Mr. Bishop explained. "We do this first, by informing the public what it can expect to find on next Thursday's program, and second, by telling about the artists and people who are connected with the show. Television is remarkably similar to the movies in one respect—it sparks the public interest in the personal lives of the stars and makes the audience want to know everything about them. It is a revival of the old fan interest. This was seldom true in radio where an important figure could be almost unknown to the public because he was just a voice. Not so in television, though, because now you can see the artist and even a minor star who has been in television can attract attention on a street when the public recognizes her.

"In brief—we satisfy personal curiosity of what the program and the people are like, our object being to make more people tune in on our band or channel. Today, the newspapers are almost entirely interested in television news, not radio, and we must fulfill that requirement."

In addition to routine press releases which are issued each day to cover advance shows, special releases are prepared to tell about the forthcoming "spectaculars"—a descriptive term for the hour-and-a-half shows which feature a bevy of stars as well as spectacular scenery and staging. One problem in publicizing many of the shows is that artists are cast only two or three weeks prior to the actual performance and that gives little time to prepare the releases and service the press. Releases are sent all over the country to newspapers in every city where the program is televised as well as to many neighboring towns. The flow of information is principally out of New York and Hollywood. Copies of every release sent to papers are furnished the manager of each local station so he knows what his papers have received. He handles publicity mainly for local programs that originate at his station. This enables him to concentrate largely on his programs.

Although we have mentioned the press photographers in passing, we did not mean to minimize the importance of pictures. If you are a "shutter bug" and interested in public relations too, you should know something about the photography section. Nine photographers, including the darkroom technicians, cover all the shows and take pictures either in their own portrait studios or at the program studio. Occasionally a photographer is required to take pictures in an artist's home or to cover a special news assignment that should bring publicity for the company or one of its stars. Each week five pictures are served to every major newspaper with a special service of three to about fifty larger papers. Thus a total of eight pictures is sent to those papers where more space is available for pictures.

"Despite the fact that editors like to see pictures and they are in great demand, out of a total of eight pictures serviced to a paper, we cannot expect to place more than two or three," Mr. Bishop explained. "The competition is keen and so we must keep plugging away constantly."

To qualify for this work you must be an experienced professional photographer. New members of the staff must work first in the darkroom before they receive picture assignments.

When we talked with Mr. Bishop, he mentioned that he was temporarily detached from his regular assignment to concentrate on exploiting the spectacular programs which required an extra push because of their size, importance, and cost. At the same time he was trying to develop ways of using one program to promote another by introducing a special stunt or mention which would call attention to a coming show.

As part of his promotion for "Best Foot Forward," Mr. Bishop invited a man who taught baton twirling to Connecticut high school girls to bring sixteen of his pupils to New York to appear on the morning Dave Garroway show. To the tune of "Buckle Down Winsocki," a hit tune from the show, the gayly costumed twirlers twirled their fastest in front of the windows of the RCA Exhibition Hall, home of Dave Garroway's "Today" program. But this was not all! Mr. Bishop notified all stations carrying the Dave Garroway show that the twirlers were coming and suggested that each station manager invite his local baton twirlers to come in and do the same locally—all to the tune of "Buckle Down Winsocki." The idea caught on like wildfire and "Best Foot Forward" got its full measure of publicity.

The day we saw Mr. Bishop he was working with R. H. Macy & Company, New York's largest department store, on a joint promotion for the spectacular "Babes in Toyland." In return for furnishing the toys to be used in the show and having its name appear on the stage set, Macy's agreed to share the cost of joint newspaper ads announcing the show—as well as the fact that Macy's is the place to buy toys. For added promotion Mr. Bishop was trying to have the Macy's employee choir assemble in the toy department to sing selections from "Babes in Toyland" for the Dave Garroway show.

NBC requires applicants to have three years of newspaper experience to qualify for a position in the press department. "We need staff writers who can discover, create, and polish off a good story in such a manner that it will be ready for the editor to print," Mr. Bishop said. "He doesn't have to know how to plant it, we have machinery to take care of that, but he must know how to roll up his sleeves and produce usable copy. Local stations employ one or more people to handle their publicity and since there are more than 3,500 radio and television stations in the country, you can see that there is a good opportunity for those interested in doing writing and publicity for the radio and TV industry."

Mr. Bishop has not severed all his ties with the South! Although he thinks newspaper work is one-tenth excitement and nine-tenths dull routine, he writes a weekly column, "Dixie All Over," which he has syndicated in five North Carolina newspapers. "The home folks probably have the impression that my only activity is hunting down natives of the Tar Heel State who are in New York," Mr. Bishop chuckled. As for us—we went away wondering when he found time to do his column!

The Metropolitan Opera Association

It was just four days before the opening of the 1954-55 season of the Met when we stopped at the box office and asked for Francis Robinson, assistant manager of the Metropolitan Opera Association. Yes, we had an appointment with Mr. Robinson, and two minutes later he was at the front door.

"Perhaps you would first like to look in on a dress rehearsal," he suggested and a moment later we sank luxuriously into a rear orchestra seat to watch part of the second act of *Andrea Chenier*. Later he led the way to his office which opens just off the main foyer. As we entered, the phone was ringing. "Would television cameras be permitted in Sherry's restaurant on opening night?" Another call followed—"Could he possibly attend a meeting that evening?" A third call—and then he suggested that we go to his uptown apartment where we could talk undisturbed. Four days to go—but this key man, second in command, was nevertheless willing and anxious to take time out to talk with us and pass on helpful advice for those interested in following in his footsteps.

Mr. Robinson has a kindly face and speaks with a faint suggestion of a southern accent. A Kentuckian by birth, he grew up in Tennessee, and attended Vanderbilt University. Following graduation he spent five years as a newspaper reporter before he was brought to New York by William Fields, press representative for the Playrights' Company, the year that organization was formed. Soon he found himself acting as company manager for Katharine Cornell and later her press representative. Intermittently he also served as press representative for Cornelia Otis Skinner, Guthrie McClintic, Theatre, Inc., and Edwin Lester's production of *Song of Norway*. In the year that S. Hurok booked the company, Mr. Robinson had full responsibility for the annual tour of the Metropolitan Opera. He came to the Metropolitan full time in 1948.

In 1950 Rudolph Bing, the new general manager of the Metropolitan Opera House, engaged Mr. Robinson to take charge of the box office and the all-important opera subscriptions as well as the tour. Two years later he became assistant manager. His duties are now expanded to include all contacts with the press and under his supervision there is a staff of ten in the box office plus three for the press department.

Mr. Robinson thinks of the Metropolitan Opera as a company rather than as some ninety individual artists plus an orchestra of eighty top musicians. Actually its level of artistic excellence, which Mr. Robinson believes is unexcelled anywhere in the world, is the best possible kind of public relations.

"Public relations is everyone's job, not just that of an individual or a department," Mr. Robinson declared. "We do not need a special man or department to push the idea. Everyone connected with our organization is instinctively public relations conscious."

"How then," we asked, "would you refer to yourself when dealing with the press?"

"I prefer to be called press representative," he answered, "because I work closely with the three principal means of communication—the press, radio, and television. My main purpose, of course, is to sell the Metropolitan Opera."

One of the regular duties of Mr. Robinson's staff during the opera season is to send the newspapers advance releases of the repertoire for the coming week. This is news eagerly awaited by music lovers all over the country and is always sure to command a good part of a column in the leading New York newspapers. As need arises or a good story develops, additional releases are issued and his staff handles special assignments in addition to answering many, many letters that come to the Met from all parts of the world.

Mr. Robinson is more reserved in his approach to promotion than the average press representative or agent. Even his personality reflects the dignity and tradition of the opera and you can sense the fact that he will never compromise that dignity in order to get cheap publicity.

To understand his approach you must remember that the Metropolitan Opera, founded in 1883, is known and loved throughout the nation. Since 1932 it has received financial support from thousands of music lovers and in 1940, when the opera house was about to be sold, friends from all over the country came to its rescue, its vast radio audience contributing one-third of the necessary funds and the Opera Guild the balance. Its music has been broadcast to millions of homes every Saturday afternoon for years and its artists proudly associate their name with the Metropolitan when they appear elsewhere in public. In 1954 the opening performance was televised in 32 theaters throughout the country. The Metropolitan Opera House belongs to America; it is truly part of America.

We asked Mr. Robinson if in view of his conservative approach to his job he had enjoyed any unusual publicity windfalls. "Yes," he said, "Marian Anderson provided us with a big story."

Miss Anderson had been meeting with Maestro Dimitri Mitropoulos and the latter telephoned Mr. Bing that they had reached an agreement whereby Miss Anderson would sing in *The Masked Ball* at the Metropolitan during the 1954-55 season. Mr. Bing then called Mr. Hurok, Miss Anderson's manager, told him that Mr. Robinson had prepared a very short press release, and asked where Miss Anderson might be found. At first it was feared she had gone shopping and could not be found but someone learned that she was due at her accompanist's studio at two o'clock that afternoon. As soon as he heard this, Mr. Robinson put the wheels in motion for a press conference in Mr. Bing's office later that afternoon. Mr. Hurok brought Miss Anderson to the Opera House whereupon she signed the contract in the presence of the thirteen photographers and numerous reporters who had turned out to cover the story of the first Negro singer to join the Metropolitan Opera Association. Nationwide press and magazine coverage resulted, for this was a real news story that even the European papers featured.

We tell this story because it illustrates Mr. Robinson's idea of press relations. He calls in reporters only when he has a big story but handles it with restraint and in such a way that he does not violate the traditions of this great American institution.

"What advice would you give a young man or woman

who wanted to be press representative for a famous musician, singer, artist, or actor?" we asked Mr. Robinson.

"A good education is essential, particularly in the liberal arts. Anything and everything you know can help you in this business. Newspaper work is almost essential because not only do you learn how the press works, but you learn to think and work quickly—and under pressure. Actually I think you must have a flair or knack for this kind of work, just as a writer of poetry or a novelist must have special innate ability in his field.

"I always loved the theater, it was hard to stop me!" he said in answer to our question asking how he got into the Metropolitan. The same goes for *you* too! If you hope to get into the world of music or the theater, let nothing stop you. "Get your newspaper experience," says Mr. Robinson, "get to know people who are in the business and try to come to the notice of those whom you would serve."

Sports

The world of sports offers exciting opportunities to those of you who are sports fans and interested in public relations. Look at the sporting pages of any major metropolitan daily and you will see how much news about sports is needed every day of the year to fill the public's insatiable appetite for this type of reading. Promotion or publicity agents serve major leagues, ball clubs, race tracks, prize fighters and other prominent professional athletes and athletic teams. The publicity is designed to keep the name of the team or individual before the public eye and also to pep up attendance at games or contests. This is one business where you would work closely with the press.

Suppose, for a moment, that you were public relations or publicity director for a major ball club. Prior to a game you would make necessary arrangements for receiving and possibly entertaining distinguished guests or patrons. Another of your responsibilities would be to see that the press box is in order. Little details like pencils and pads for each reporter—important matters such as making sure everything is in order for the radio and TV men who cover the game. Then, once the game is in progress, you would give the reporters a running commentary full of statistical information and background material on the game. After the game, you would handle any special requests the reporters might make, check on the departure of distinguished visitors, and attend to any public relations problems that might arise.

As the ball players travel, you would naturally keep your eyes open to see that the sports writers who follow the team were comfortable and happy. You would feed to the press a constant stream of information about your players, statistics on their performance, and biographical and human interest stories that would help to keep your ball club in the limelight. You would also answer correspondence from the public and requests for information about the club and its players. In other words, you would richly earn the long vacation that comes at the end of the season.

Familiarity with the sport and its jargon, plus newspaper experience as a sports writer, are essential requirements for anyone interested in this work.

CHAPTER

12

Public Relations in Publishing

Harper & Brothers

"Doing publicity in a publishing house is not the glamour job most young people imagine. It's mostly routine and hard work." That is the gist of what Ramona Herdman told us when we talked shop in her office. She has been Harper's publicity director for twenty-five years, so we suspect that Miss Herdman speaks with authority.

Miss Herdman, who is vivacious as well as stimulating, was born and raised in Greenwich, New York, and entered Syracuse University to take a liberal arts course—with a vague notion that she might like to do newspaper work. When she learned that the School of Journalism was just starting, she immediately registered for all the courses she was permitted to take. Shortly thereafter, at the suggestion of one of her professors, she entered a $200 prize contest sponsored by the Syracuse *Journal* for the best news story written by a student. Her story was judged best because it was short and usable just as it was submitted. This success prompted her to transfer to the School of Journalism and at the end of her sophomore year the Syracuse *Herald* offered a part-time reporting job to "the girl who won the *Journal* prize." The next two years Miss

Herdman attended the university and worked as a reporter after classes. The Rochester *Post Express* learned of her and bid for her services but kept her for only a year because the *Herald* lured her back.

Five years later Miss Herdman decided to take a year's leave of absence to do some more studying in New York at Columbia and to write feature stories for the *Herald*. At the same time she did feature stories for the Sunday *World*, conducted publicity for the Salvation Army's fund raising campaign, and worked for the New York State League of Women Voters. It was during this time that she met Ruth Raphael who was in charge of publicity at Harper's. "Miss Raphael was the smartest publicity director I had ever met—and a swell person too!" Miss Herdman observed.

The Syracuse Health Commissioner made Miss Herdman such an attractive offer to do publicity for the Health Department and the Milbank Foundation Health Demonstration that she found herself once more back in Syracuse. But less than a year later she resigned to accept a job at about half the salary as assistant to the woman she admired so much—Miss Raphael of Harper's. Before the year was out, Miss Raphael was promoted to another position and Miss Herdman was placed in charge of publicity, a post she has held ever since.

"Nothing is publicity unless people read about it, hear about it, or see it," Miss Herdman observed. "Merely turning out hundreds of press releases, pictures, and other promotional material does not constitute publicity unless at least some of it is used. The amount of money wasted on paper, envelopes, and stamps in sending stacks of releases to newspapers of this country is appalling when so much of it ends up in the wastebasket."

For this reason Miss Herdman emphasizes the importance of learning something about newspapers before trying to tackle a publicity job in a publishing house. "If possible, a student should get a job on a small newspaper during the summer because she will see exactly what happens when a release arrives and how a newspaper operates. Large city papers are so departmentalized that you cannot see at first-hand how news is handled."

Take releases about new books, for instance. What could seem more pointless than to send indiscriminately releases and even copies of books to editors all over the country, hoping that they will run a story. Yet it happens every day and Miss Herdman has been in many newspaper offices where the shelves are filled with new books that were never even opened. Why? Because that newspaper didn't even have a book review column! Do you understand why Miss Herdman thinks newspaper experience is valuable?

The problem of having one's books reviewed is real indeed, particularly when you learn that The New York *Times Book Review* receives each year 7,500 books and finds room to review but 2,500. These figures exclude technical, text, foreign, and privately printed books which are practically never reviewed.

At Harper's, advertising and sales promotion is a separate department from publicity. The chief responsibility of the publicity department is to get publicity for the firm's books. The first step in publicizing a book is to prepare and issue news releases before publication. This is routine and automatic. Next, review copies must be sent to the right editors. They are chosen with care and each book goes to a different list. They are never sent out broadside. Samples of illustrations, or, if the book has none, a picture of the jacket design and the author's photograph go to the right people. Finally, the author is consulted to see if he can be useful in a personal way—in radio interviews, appearing before women's clubs, as the subject of feature columns, etc. An author can always be presented in the local community through newspaper interviews and possibly on a suitable radio or TV program.

"Every book requires a separate and different publicity job," Miss Herdman said. "First, we try to get reviews; then, we try to call the book to the attention of people who might want to buy it." In addition to promoting the firm's books, Miss Herdman, her assistant, and her secretary serve as a clearing house for information about Harper's, answer inquiries from the press, radio, and TV, and try to keep up with the constant stream of requests for material on authors, book lists, and a hundred and one other subjects.

"Publicity can be a very discouraging business too," Miss Herdman warns. "Every year thousands of books are published but only a small number are reviewed in any one newspaper. Except for the newspapers with regular book sections such as the New York *Times*, the New York *Herald Tribune*, the Chicago *Tribune*, etc., even papers that do review books cover but a very limited number and are highly selective at that. It is the height of folly to expect an editor to print a news story about a book unless there is something unusual about the author or the book that makes for genuine news. It is bad public relations to send news releases that contain no news, for they waste the editor's time, and he eventually learns to ignore your releases altogether."

Despite the fact that every June many applicants apply for the available jobs, the right type of person seldom comes along, according to Miss Herdman. Most of them vaguely say that they want to do publicity. Few of them come with any skills; in fact, a secretary straight from secretarial school with typing, shorthand, and clerical skills could have a better chance of getting a beginning job at publicity than the best English major.

"I would advise a young person interested in doing publicity for a publisher to get a job on a local newspaper. But because a person comes to me with newspaper experience," Miss Herdman cautioned, "doesn't necessarily mean he will make a good publicity assistant. Too many starry-eyed young people who have taken English and journalism courses and worked on their college newspaper think that our job is mostly a matter of writing and sending out publicity releases, meeting authors, and dropping in on literary teas. Far from it! The work is often discouraging, the endless routine is sometimes irksome but it is always terrifically challenging!"

Let's leave the venerable publishing house of Harper and Brothers, which has been in business since 1817, and travel up Madison Avenue to drop in at a young firm that specializes in an entirely different type of publishing.

Paperbound Books

No doubt you have often stood in a drugstore fascinated by the display of paperbound books. Your eyes darted here, there, and back again, as the colorful and bizarre covers with their equally captivating titles claimed your attention. But in this welter of popular science, mysteries, crime and passion, perhaps you were surprised to find a large section of serious titles too—for such there are.

Paperbound books are the lifeblood of the New American Library of World Literature which reprints fiction and nonfiction in its Signet, Signet Key, and Mentor Book series. The quality of the reprints issued by this publisher is on the whole unusually high. Under the Signet imprint, good fiction is issued with a few mysteries, westerns, science fiction and nonfiction titles included too. Signet Key books concentrate on titles in the "how to," self-improvement, and informational categories. Reprints in the Mentor series range in subject matter from anthropology, psychology, and economics to classics and the arts.

The promotion manager who is responsible for all the firm's promotion and advertising is the attractive and personable Miss Jay Tower. Bookcases that line one wall of her office offer an eye-dazzling array of the firm's books while, on the opposite side of the room, a long bulletin board displays colorful examples of special promotional pieces.

"We handle promotion, publicity, and advertising in this department," Miss Tower explained, "and that includes about a dozen new titles every month." In order to understand better what Miss Tower and her staff of five do, you should know that 90 per cent of the paperbound books (unlike most hard cover books) are distributed through wholesalers, who in turn handle the distribution to the newsstands, drugstores, paper stores, supermarkets, etc. Therefore, a paperbound house concentrates a lot of promotion on the wholesaler and gets him squarely behind the book instead of worrying about the drugstore clerk or the newsdealer who is seldom if ever contacted.

Miss Tower lists the following as her chief responsibilities:

1. Promotion

Promotion includes planning brochures, circulars, flyers, catalogs, and order forms that are designed and printed to interest both the trade (wholesalers, bookstores, etc.) and the consumers (who include professors, librarians, and individuals) in the titles of any particular publishing house. These come in a tremendous variety of sizes, shapes, colors and different kinds of presentations. The comprehensive catalog, which lists all the firm's books and is issued four times a year, is also an important promotional activity.

2. Publicity

The usual publicity program for a book starts when Miss Tower talks with the author to see what press, radio and TV publicity may be obtained. For most reprints this type of publicity is not possible because when the book was originally printed, the usual publicity channels were well worked over. Now and then, however, an important or timely reprint will warrant trying for wide publicity.

3. Advertising

"Advertising is not as important to the reprint house as to the hardcover publisher," Miss Tower said. "It was only last year that we took our first full page in the New York *Times Book Review.* Occasionally we run an ad in *Publishers' Weekly* or *The Saturday Review,* but we know that money is best spent when put into promotional material that will encourage the wholesaler to push our books. For this reason the art and copy work on our covers are of extreme importance. We depend on impulse buying and the point of sale is reached when the prospective buyer's eyes are finally attracted by one cover that stands out and almost reaches up to him. Even the publishers of hard cover books recognize the psychological importance of attractive jackets but of course they are not as dependent on the lure of the jacket to sell their books since they lean more heavily on advertising."

4. Cover Copy

Preparation of the cover copy includes writing the selling copy on the front and back covers of the books, and the all-important "page one," which briefly tells something about the content of the book. This is a point of sales copy aimed only at the consumer.

5. Special Promotion

Special promotion is undertaken when the subject matter of a book seems to justify the effort and expense. "Here's a job we did on *The Execution of Private Slovak,*" she said. "It will give you an idea of how that sort of thing is done.

"First, we sent this large printed telegram to hundreds of key bookstores, and since we rarely contact them, this gimmick undoubtedly made an impression. Then we prepared these bright and unusual 'teasers' to be sent to the wholesalers. You can see that they are designed to excite their interest and curiosity in the book."

Holding up a colorfully printed card: "These are book-rack cards for use in the stores where the books are sold. We furnish them to the wholesaler who urges the dealers in the bookstores to put them up in the store. Here are some large display cards we prepared for use in Detroit, the home of Private Slovak, and in Philadelphia, headquarters for the 28th Division of which he was a member.

"There were a thousand and one local angles to exploit. We sent releases to local papers all over the country; in fact, wherever anyone who was mentioned in the book lived. Newspapers picked up these releases, interviewed the people mentioned, and gave us an excellent press. In Detroit there was a fight between the various papers—they were all trying to scoop each other! In Washington we contacted people who had figured in the book and who were still around and got several good stories. The history of this promotion ends here," she said. She smiled and held up a copy of *Look* magazine which ran a condensation of the book.

Miss Tower grew up in New Rochelle, New York, and went to Smith College where she majored in English but took as many other courses as possible "to find out what was going on." Following graduation she came to New York to work for Appleton-Century but after four years in Northampton, Massachusetts, she found city life distasteful, so she went on to New Haven and then to Boston, doing a variety of things including some writing. Eventually she landed back in New York, which she now found more tolerable, and took a secretarial job at Doubleday. "I was completely brazen," she admitted, laughing. "It was mostly a matter of relying on my memory and a fumbling kind of shorthand, but Ken McCormick, who was then chief associate editor, was very tolerant." From there she transferred to the editorial department of the Literary Guild where she read books and did layouts for the Guild's monthly magazine, *Wings*.

Month after month Miss Tower watched the Book-of-the-Month Club get more publicity than the Literary Guild. Finally she could stand it no longer and wrote a long memo to her boss about publicity and the Literary Guild. As a result the publishers considered hiring Edward Bernays to handle their publicity but gave Miss Tower a chance to try out her ideas. Result—for the next ten years she devoted her time to publicity and a miscellany of other jobs concerned with *Wings*, the Literary Guild, and the other book clubs that Doubleday sponsored. Eventually she left Doubleday to tackle her present assignment because she wanted to try something new.

Miss Tower still finds time for tennis, swimming, the theater, and her other interests and friends, thus managing to lead a well-balanced life. "People who are in the publishing business are in it by choice," she said. "They find the work congenial, they are congenial to each other and therefore they tend to make their friends within the profession. Unfortunately, there is a limit on what editors can pay for publicity and anyone looking for big money should go elsewhere."

"How would you advise a girl who is anxious to do publicity for a publisher?" we asked. Without hesitating, Miss Tower replied: "She should learn to be a good secretary. That is an absolutely certain way to get into the business and, given the right background and interest in the field, she can get herself into an essential position. Later, if she has the proper qualifications and shows a real desire to do publicity, she has a good chance to break into the publicity department."

"But what about the men, are there no opportunities for them in your field?"

"As a matter of fact," Miss Tower said, "there are many men in this profession, perhaps 40 per cent of the publicity directors are men. You must remember, though, that the margin of profit in publishing is small and salaries therefore are lower than the average prevailing scales. You find women in most of the jobs because they can manage to live on a smaller salary than a married man with a family."

"How would a man get into publicity?" we asked next.

Miss Tower laughed. "Certainly not as a secretary! He would have to get his promotional experience elsewhere and then switch jobs to a publishing firm which had an opening on its staff and could pay him a large enough salary."

Doubleday's Trainee Program

Doubleday and Company offers a practical solution for college graduates anxious to find their niche in publishing. Under its trainee program, each June Doubleday interviews the most promising college graduates and then selects ten for its trainee group. Men and women are eligible but a higher percentage of women are chosen because the turnover among the fair sex is faster and they can be used in more beginning jobs.

A liberal arts degree is the only college background required. A mastery of shorthand and typing is also necessary if you are not a man, but Doubleday will keep positions open for successful applicants while they acquire these skills. There is presently no formal program for trainees. They go from department to department as needed and learn all angles of the publishing business until there is an opening in the special division in which they are interested. Thereupon they are given a permanent assignment on a junior executive level.

Public Relations and the Press

Newspapers rarely have a conscious public relations program because their activity is of a public relations nature. Without intending a pun, we might say that newspapers are very much in the public eye and their good (or bad) deeds are readily apparent. The way they conduct their business, the manner in which they handle news stories, pictures and editorials, is their public relations. Unlike almost any other activity, newspapers cannot ask or persuade others to tell about their good deeds since they are the major media for carrying releases and news stories. Therefore, a newspaper is limited to creating special promotions.

Leaving aside the type of promotion that is an out and out circulation booster such as contests, puzzles, "lucky bucks," and other gimmicks, we find certain promotions that merely serve to impress upon the public that the newspaper is a good citizen. Examples are the New York Herald Tribune Fresh Air Fund, the New York Times Hundred Neediest Cases, and the Chicago Tribune Theater of the Air.

The public relations or promotion department, in addition to handling special promotions, sends news releases about its own activities to appropriate trade publications (a story about a new fleet of delivery trucks would go to all automotive periodicals), prepares speech material and biographies for members of the organization, and may undertake miscellaneous chores that are not the responsibility of other departments.

Like newspapers, the wire services (Associated Press, United Press, International News Service) and the syndicates (services which sell comic strips, feature stories, fiction, gossip columns, etc.) have similar promotion problems but offer on the whole a very limited field for someone interested in practicing public relations.

Newspaper experience is a necessary prerequisite for this type of work and it is a field dominated by males—as is the entire newspaper business. A public relations or promotion department may become a one-man show as a reporter is selected to head up that function. We would suggest that for the time being you do not give this activity too much thought. If you serve your apprenticeship on a newspaper, you will have an opportunity to observe the public relations needs of your paper and we believe that you will probably elect to seek a public relations contact that has a better defined and broader area of responsibility.

Magazines

Magazines, like newspapers, are media for carrying publicity but they are not of the day-to-day type like newspapers and their contents have a semi-permanent value. Since magazines have national circulation, they cannot be identified with a single community and establish themselves as good citizens like a newspaper. They often perform useful services to the public by publishing articles that expose a fraud or danger to society and thus bring about change and benefit to the public. Most of their promotions are for the purpose of building up circulation.

Frequently when a magazine is about to run an unusual story its publicity office will service the press with a release containing a digest of the article and perhaps even a tear sheet with permission to extract a certain number of words. Publicity about forthcoming articles and their authors is also sent to the columnists and press.

Here too, prior newspaper experience would be required, and women will find that some jobs are open to them in this field.

CHAPTER

13

Public Relations Counsel

So far in our discussion of public relations we have told of men and women who are employed by a corporation or an organization to plan and carry out its program of public relations, promotion or publicity, as the case may be. Just as some companies do not employ lawyers on their staff but use outside counsel when they require legal advice, many business concerns and organizations hire public relations counsel to help them with their public relations problems or to establish a public relations program. In such cases the organization employing outside public relations counsel may or may not have a public relations department of its own.

A public relations counselor is an individual who is especially qualified by training and experience to counsel others on public relations problems as well as to plan and undertake the proper public relations program that will adequately meet the client's needs. Professional public relations counseling firms range in size from one-man shops to the largest that employ upwards of three hundred people.

We have already noted that in New York City alone there are almost 500 public relations counselors listed in the phone book. A few of the best known and largest firms include Carl

Byoir Associates, Dudley, Anderson & Yutzy, Steve Hannagan Associates, Hill and Knowlton, Edward L. Bernays, and Ivy Lee & T. J. Ross (see Chapter 2). Unfortunately there are some self-styled public relations counselors who are not worthy of the title. They may be quacks who have little or no idea of what public relations is or they may be individuals who have been exposed to public relations for a short time and therefore consider themselves qualified to counsel others on their problems.

A public relations counseling organization may act merely in a consulting capacity to management or it may give advice and also help establish a public relations department within the company and continue to act as consultant to both management and the newly formed department. On the other hand, it may be retained to conduct all of the public relations activities for a company or merely to handle occasional, emergency, or unusual job assignments.

What, you ask, is the advantage of retaining professional public relations counsel, particularly if a company has its own public relations staff? Here are the principal reasons for using such a firm:

1. A small company that could not afford its own public relations department can obtain expert help.

2. A large company that has its own public relations department can call upon a public relations counselor for assistance in solving special problems. An independent counselor can approach a problem without prejudice and see it from a fresh and objective viewpoint.

3. A professional public relations firm brings broad experience and knowledge to solve a problem because its staff members have had a variety of training and experience.

4. A public relations counselor can be entirely unbiased and independent in making recommendations to manage-

ment. He need not worry about "office politics" or the risk of antagonizing the boss.

5. A professional public relations firm can provide very specialized press coverage as well as expert handling of other media. It is also in a position to furnish ghost-written articles which can be placed in the proper channels.

Public relations counseling organizations generally are managed by the partners or owners of the firm who line up their clients and mastermind the basic planning of the solution to be applied to the problem. Under the partners serves a staff of account executives. Each of these experienced men is assigned one or more accounts for which he is responsible. Working under the general direction of a partner he may call upon other staff members for advice and help. Staff members do not usually specialize; however, specialists are hired when the need arises or the size of the firm warrants it.

This being an age of specialization, we find public relations organizations that specialize in community relations, financial relations, labor relations, shareholder relations, company publications, fund raising, etc. One of the newest developments in this field struck us as being so unusual and fascinating that we pause to tell you about it.

Burdick-Rowland Associates, Inc.

"We're unique—no one else has had the nerve to try it," George M. Rowland, Jr. of Burdick-Rowland Associates, Inc. told us as we discussed the role of the modern public relations counselor. "We specialize in visual promotions and three-dimensional public relations because we have the experience and know-how to counsel in that field. Practically everything we do is of a visual nature that supplements the work of established public relations counselors or the public relations department of a corporate client."

Walking through the large room that houses the design

department we saw what he meant. On all sides were plans and designs for exhibits, displays, shadow boxes and many other modern eye-catching devices depicting ideas that are the stock-in-trade of this unusual firm. We were particularly fascinated by one animated miniature display that would serve as the prototype of the real thing which soon would be bringing an important message from a prominent corporation to the public.

Burdick-Rowland Associates is perhaps best known for its handling of the broker window displays sponsored by the New York Stock Exchange. Twelve nationally known companies whose stocks are listed on the New York Stock Exchange agreed in 1954 to have specially designed and animated exhibits installed in the ground floor windows of 45 brokerage houses in 47 cities throughout the Northeast section of the country. The exhibits, designed and produced by Burdick-Rowland Associates, show the part played by American industry in our free-enterprise system and it is planned eventually to place these and additional exhibits in nearly 300 different locations all over the country. Custom-built trucks and crews of specially trained men move and install the exhibits which remain in each location for only twenty-eight days. This entire operation is under the guidance of an executive who is a specialist in traffic, transportation, scheduling, and routing. The sign on the door of his office appropriately reads: "Nuts and Bolts Department." What with exacting deadlines, show dates, the necessity of keeping 144 exhibits maintained and moved from city to city and coast to coast every 28 days, a sense of humor is essential at Burdick-Rowland.

Other activities of the firm are just as unusual and interesting. With the emphasis on the visual presentation, they have included such projects as helping top management of several large corporations plan and conduct their annual shareholders' meetings, planning all details for sales meetings, developing symbols, trade marks, sales identifiers, designing reception rooms and offices, running conventions and open houses, and creating the permanent exhibit of the Sun Oil Company at the Franklin Institute in Philadelphia.

The staff includes the partners, the head designer and his four assistants, supervisor of the "Nuts and Bolts Department," the manager of a West Coast office, and accounting, clerical, and stenographic personnel.

Edward H. Burdick is an architect by profession. The displays that he designed for the Chicago World's Fair, the New York World's Fair and the San Francisco Treasure Island Fair and his work as director of exhibits for the Federal government at these fairs won him much fame. Perhaps he is best known for his pioneering in the field of diorama and for designing and expediting the famous Freedom Train in 1947, planning the Civil Defense "Alert America" Cavalcade that toured America in 1952, and designing the financial exhibits for the gallery of the New York Stock Exchange. His is the idea of the Broker Window Plan.

When Rowland was in college he was careful to choose those courses which would best prepare him to become a writer. Upon graduation, he realized his ambition by becoming a reporter for the Hearst newspapers. After advancing to promotion manager and space salesman, he successively opened an advertising agency, ran his own newspaper, and served as advertising manager of a utility and a department store. He then started as a salesman for Gardner Displays Company and eventually became executive vice-president in charge of sales and design, and for three years ran the coast-to-coast sales meetings for a large corporation. In this capacity he designed all exhibits and displays, prepared speeches, wrote scripts for the stage shows, managed a theatrical troupe, arranged for all luncheons and housing, co-ordinated publicity and constantly worried about the two baggage cars crammed full of props and displays. He also learned considerably more about theatrical unions than he had in his avocation of managing amateur theatrical troupes.

Most recently he served on the staff of the American Museum of Natural History in New York as general manager in charge of television, radio, films, membership, retail sales, catering and cafeterias, membership campaigns, lectures, etc. In 1953 he and Mr. Burdick joined hands to form the firm that bears their names. They are both firmly convinced that in time this specialized knowledge of three-dimensional selling will achieve a professional status not now acknowledged because it is so new. Certainly you can see that this concept will open new vistas for young people—particularly those who have real artistic ability and some training in that field.

In Conclusion

As you may have guessed, public relations counseling represents a development in the profession that calls for men and women who have had heavy experience in public relations or three to five years of newspaper experience, and who are capable of taking on an assignment and seeing it through to completion. It therefore offers few if any job possibilities for young people just entering the field.

We mention counseling, however, because you should know about this important part of public relations and how it too serves. After you have received your training and experience you may find it advantageous to join such a firm, but first concentrate on getting a few years of practical public relations experience under your belt!

CHAPTER

14

Public Relations at Work

In the preceding chapters we have seen examples of the need for public relations in business, publishing, government, social agencies, schools and colleges, etc. We have touched on problems peculiar to each of these activities and how public relations has often been the means of successfully solving them, as well as improving the relationships between the impersonal organization and its public.

We should now go from the general to the specific, from an over-all discussion of what public relations does, to specific examples of how public relations is actually conducted. Despite all its glamour, public relations is hard work, but for those who like it, the most fascinating job imaginable. Perhaps you can better draw your own conclusions after you have spent a day with one of the country's leading public relations directors.

MEET DORCAS CAMPBELL

"My job is the most interesting one in the bank," says Dorcas Campbell, vivacious and petite assistant vice-president of the East River Savings Bank in New York. And after you've learned what this famous woman does we think you'll readily agree.

Just by way of background, Miss Campbell is a Hoosier by birth and a New Yorker by adoption. Even before attending the University of Michigan, Miss Campbell did social service publicity but decided to enter the university to take courses in journalism and determine whether or not she wanted a lifetime of that profession. Between semesters she made a flying visit to New York at the request of a friend, Mr. Darwin James, the former president of the social agency where she had worked. He was now president of the East River Savings Bank and wanted her to join the staff to handle a new kind of service department for customers. It was to prove a milestone in banking history. Despite her lack of banking knowledge, she accepted the job—and the challenge. It was not long afterwards that the woman who handled the bank's advertising and the five service departments left, and Miss Campbell was assigned these added responsibilities. Later, during 1943, in recognition of the outstanding job she had done, Miss Campbell was elected an officer of the East River Savings Bank, a unique distinction among the savings banks in metropolitan New York. As director of public relations, which includes responsibility for the bank's entire publicity and advertising program and direction of the service departments, some 20 employees, scattered through the five offices, report to Miss Campbell. Her keen judgment and business acumen are sought daily by almost every department in the bank.

Miss Campbell's reputation stems not only from the many imaginative and unusual ideas she has introduced to the field of banking, but from her uncanny ability (when teaching or writing about her favorite subject) to breathe new life into banking and give it as much glamour as aviation or TV. She has lectured on public relations and banking at the Financial

Public Relations School at Northwestern University. She gave a course in public relations at the New York University School of Commerce and organized and led a course on "Women and Their Money" at the New School for Social Research. Her books and many articles on banking have established her as an authority in the field.

Let's join Miss Campbell as she walks briskly into the bank on Cortlandt Street, close to the heart of New York's busy financial district. Her office is tucked away at one end of the impressive banking floor and we take a seat in a corner where we can see and hear everything that goes on.

The mail is the first business of the day. Fortunately it is light today—several letters from customers complimenting the bank on its service, one letter of complaint, two letters from other banks involving routine business, a request to make a speech before a large women's club, a letter from a university asking if Miss Campbell would consider teaching a course in banking, three letters presenting different promotional ideas, and from the Girl Scouts of America a couple of reports to read and checks to sign. She was elected their treasurer in 1951.

Next, the daily reminder file is checked to see what jobs must be tackled today. Miss Campbell says she is too busy and has too much on her mind to rely on her memory. Instead, something to be done on a certain day is noted in the reminder file. Today there is a reminder to plan for the next issue of *The Log*, an attractive but inexpensive promotional piece the size of a post card, which each month brings to depositors a cheerful and unusual slant on savings or news of the bank.

Miss Campbell may dictate to her secretary or on her dictation machine as she acknowledges the complimentary letters and tactfully explains to the man who wrote the letter of complaint that the state banking regulations make it impossible to adopt his suggestion. The two letters received from banks are routed to appropriate department heads with a brief note on each. A letter of regret is dictated to the women's club because Miss Campbell has already accepted a speaking engagement at a fund raising drive for the same day. The letter from the university is tucked in her brief case to take home for further thought.

The telephone rings, bringing the distressing news that one of the trustees of the bank is very ill and has just been taken to the hospital. Miss Campbell immediately telephones the hospital to check on his condition, then tells the president what she has learned. She personally calls her florist specifying what flowers are to be sent, she sets up machinery to keep a check on the trustee's progress, and—just in case—she checks his file and makes sure his biography is complete and up to date. As she makes these arrangements Miss Campbell signs the checks.

Turning to the promotional letters, she studies each carefully, trying to determine whether she should kill the idea there and then or submit it to the manager of one of the bank's offices for his opinion. "Give-aways are popular in banks today," she observed, her blue eyes twinkling. "You can see that each one of these contains an eye-catching sample of a give-away gimmick."

The phone rings. It is a friend asking if Miss Campbell would help get an increase on her mortgage. Miss Campbell calls the head of the mortgage department, then she is ready to turn to the promotional letters.

Another phone call from the secretary of the board at Girl Scout headquarters asks if Miss Campbell can attend a special officers' meeting called for that afternoon. She consults her calendar. Yes—by changing the meeting time with her staff heads she can be there. Her secretary is asked to inform the necessary people of the new meeting time.

Back to the promotional letters—but the building superintendent is at the door, asking if the American flag should not be hung outside of the building today. Miss Campbell thinks for a moment and gives her approval.

Two phone calls in succession complete arrangements for a dinner of a club at which Miss Campbell is to be a guest speaker.

At the request of a department head, the next ten minutes are spent going to the second floor to check on three large display panels which are being shipped to Washington for the Financial Public Relations convention.

Back at her desk, Miss Campbell dictates answers to two of the promotional letters and explains why the ideas are not adaptable to the bank. The third she sends to the manager of the 96th Street office with a short memo asking for his opinion.

Francis Robinson, assistant manager of the Metropolitan Opera House is on the phone. He explains an idea he has in connection with a display that is scheduled to go into the bank's six huge display windows at the strategically located Rockefeller Center office. These windows are part of the bank's regular program of showcasing the work of various groups in the community which will be of public interest. During November they are to feature a new book on the Metropolitan Opera and the display is a natural tie-in with the opening of the opera season. The bank's famous window displays are often in preparation two years in advance, demanding much time and initiative—to say nothing of ingenuity.

The idea, which involves a radio program, means that Miss Campbell must consider the merit of the suggestion, the hour of the broadcast, the number of competitors who might also have programs at the same time, the cost, and its effect on her advertising budget. She promises a decision by the end of the week and makes a note for the reminder file.

"Advertising is something like public relations," Miss Campbell remarks. "There's no sense copying what others have done. If you can't do something different or unusual that expresses the personality of your bank, it shouldn't be done."

A high-pressure space salesman for a real estate magazine confidently takes a chair by her desk to sell a half-page ad in six issues. Quickly she must consider what type of copy would pull best, the over-all cost, again what the budget could stand, and most important of all, the advantages of using this medium. Diplomatically she explains to the salesman that at the present time her budget will not permit her to undertake any additional advertising.

Another call from the Girl Scouts. This requires a policy decision which is made, and it is followed by an urgent call from the manager of the John Street office who says that he is all out of Zodiac banks. Miss Campbell frowns, for this latest brain child has proved a knotty problem ever since she introduced it. The problem is compounded by the fact that not only are there twelve zodiac signs from which interested customers may choose, but the coin banks are available in four colors as well—a total of forty-eight different varieties to stock.

"Although these coin banks sell for a dollar and a quarter each, we don't make a cent on them," she explains. "It's only a promotional deal for the benefit of those people who will save the coin bank way. Life is a matter of percentages: a percentage saves this way—a percentage saves that way. People have to trick themselves into saving the money they don't want to put aside—and we are here to help them."

Before leaving to keep a luncheon appointment with a reporter who is doing a feature story on mutual savings banks, she visits the banking floor to satisfy herself that during the busy noontime rush there has been no relaxation of the high standards set for handling new customers.

After lunch she returns to find more correspondence. Again many routine letters, several solicitations from charities, a monthly report on activity in her department at the Spring Street office and a letter, which the president referred to her for comment, suggesting that the bank advertise on a new radio network.

There is a call from a newspaper which has learned of the trustee's illness. Can the bank supply any biographical material? Yes; and she asks her publicity assistant to help the reporter.

She studies a memo prepared by a member of her staff transmitting ten form letters. These must be checked to make sure they begin with "You" and not "I," that they are written in simple understandable English, that they reflect the bank's personality and, above all, that they are courteous. "These form letters are intended as a guide for our people to follow in answering a variety of requests," Miss Campbell observes. "It is important that every letter have warmth and individuality but we do want the composition to follow along certain lines." She puts the file in her brief case, because her staff supervisors are now arriving for their meeting and there will be no other time to study the letters.

"Looks as though we can begin," Miss Campbell says, after she has greeted each of the six supervisors.

The staff meeting is concerned primarily with reviewing problems involving customer handling and customer service —some of it very technical, some very human—particularly when it comes to tracing "dormant accounts." Miss Campbell initiated the system during her first days at the bank.

Miss Campbell prefers to encourage her staff to do most of the talking and wherever possible to arrive at a satisfactory solution without her help. The number of employees who take evening banking courses at the American Institute of Banking is proof that personnel policies pay off by creating interest and enthusiasm for the job, and helps them make the right decisions. Miss Campbell is a rooter for the A.I.B.

The meeting is over and there is a telephone call from a veteran's organization asking for an advertisement from the bank for a bazaar being held. Miss Campbell explains that it is a policy of the bank that such requests must be made in writing. She hangs up the phone slowly, reflecting that the letter will require a thorough investigation of the organization and if it proves to be a worthy cause, a re-examination of the bank's policy and budget to determine whether an advertisement should be given, and, if so, how large.

Hurriedly Miss Campbell signs her mail and scoops up the magazine and trade papers that have arrived during the day and must be read at home. "Oh, the next issue of *The Log*—I never did get to it, did I!" Into her briefcase goes that file.

With a cheery farewell Miss Campbell perched her jaunty red hat on her head, grabbed her gloves, bag, and briefcase and dashed uptown for the meeting of the Girl Scout officers. Tonight after dinner she will weigh the pros and cons of the request to teach the banking course and probably dictate a reply. (She keeps a dictation machine at home so that she can work from there too!) Then she will doubtless wrestle with ideas for clever copy for *The Log*, review the ten form letters, read some of the magazines and, if time permits, perhaps do some work on her forthcoming speech. Now and then she will spot check the local radio stations to listen to her competitors' commercials—every room of her apartment being equipped with a radio since the bank first used radio as an advertising medium.

The old saying originally inspired by the overworked housewife seems to apply equally to the executive like Miss

Campbell: "Man may work from sun to sun but woman's work is never done." Miss Campbell is fortunate, for although her work is never done, you recall that she insists her job is the most interesting in the bank. And for Miss Campbell the work never will be done as long as she continues to search for ways to do a better public relations job, to broaden her contacts both in and out of banking circles, and, as a private citizen, to shoulder what she believes to be her personal responsibility to the community.

FLYING HIGH

And now let's spend a little time with another public relations executive—Jack Coneybear of American Airlines. His job has a variety of activity and here's what he has to say about it.

"My job is one that has no pattern in a business that goes on forever—twenty-four hours a day, seven days a week, continuously and without any letup," Jack Coneybear told us when we asked him what a public relations representative in an airline's public relations department did. "I sometimes work around the clock, my assignments cover a multitude of sins, and at times they almost kill me—but I love it!"

Jack Coneybear is of medium height, has dark hair and a definite twinkle in his eye. He was a resident of Westchester County, New York, until his senior year when he was transferred to high school in Oak Ridge, Tennessee. He immediately found a part-time job as disk jockey for a wired-music system that piped recorded music to nearby dance halls. Shortly thereafter he met a man who was starting a radio station in town. Offering to help and to work for nothing, Jack found himself announcing, doing news, special events, and the disk show. It was a strenuous program because he spun disks for the wired music from four until ten and then rushed to the radio station to take the ten-till-midnight shift.

Saturday he worked all day at the radio station and frequently stayed until four in the morning; however he was always back again at eight to start his Sunday stint.

While the platters were spinning he managed to do enough studying to graduate but he knew that he did not want to go on to college. What would be the sense in that, he reasoned, when already he was doing what he wanted. Wouldn't four years' experience in radio do him more good than the same time spent in college? Today, Jack realizes his mistake and firmly believes that anyone who has the opportunity to go to college should do so.

His earnings of fifty cents an hour made it necessary to return to New York to find a better paying job. Jack claims he contacted almost every radio station in New York State as well as several in New Jersey and Connecticut. Everywhere the question was the same: "What college did you attend?" Then the raised eyebrows and the inevitable: "Sorry, but we only hire men who have had college training or extensive experience in the field." Undaunted, he continued his search, meanwhile writing and trying to sell his own radio program, until nine months after graduation he finally landed a job writing news broadcasts for radio station WFAS which is owned by the Westchester County Publishers, Inc., publishers of a chain of newspapers in that county. Here he quickly found that he liked to write and had an aptitude for it.

Always interested in aviation, Jack asked if he could cover the big county air show and report it for the Monday morning broadcast. He prepared his broadcast material and also turned in a four-column story which the editor liked so much he ran it in the newspapers as a feature and gave Jack his first by-line. This proved a turning point in his career. Immediately he started looking for special stories and in addition to his radio work managed to turn out three or four a week.

An automobile accident that hospitalized him for thirteen months interrupted his career. Returning to work on crutches, Jack was confined to his desk and forced to rely on the telephone to scare up his news. One day as he was looking for a possible aviation story, he contacted his friend, Mike Wardell, American Airlines' regional director of public relations. A half hour later Mr. Wardell called him back to see if he wanted to join his public relations staff. "No, thanks," Jack told him. "I prefer newspaper work to public relations." The excitement of watching the ticker tape tap out the latest news, of rewriting the raw material for broadcasting or news articles, and best of all the thrill of sinking one's teeth into a story, prompted his refusal. But after thinking it over and discussing it further with his boss, he called Mr. Wardell back and took the job. Public relations representative with one of the largest airlines and he would not be twenty-one for another two months!

The Eastern regional public relations office covers seven states in the Eastern part of the country and twenty of the most important cities. It also includes Canada and London, England. On the director's staff are two public relations representatives and a hard-working secretary. "Flexibility rather than specialization is the important thing for us," Jack told us. "Because our staff is so small each of us must be able to do everything and cover on a minute's notice for each other."

In the field each sales manager and his staff service the local papers with releases that come to them from New York over the company's private teletype system. They handle local publicity projects themselves and it is only when something unusual occurs that they call in the experts from New York.

Jack thought for a few minutes when we asked him what he had done that morning. "I really can't remember," he said. "My two phones with their five incoming lines ring incessantly and I have been handling everything from a special reservation request for a reporter on a story to an assignment requiring me to help set up a press conference." It was obvious that too much happens too quickly so instead we asked Jack to talk about some of the assignments he had been handling recently.

"Just yesterday I flew up to Albany with two newspapermen who wanted to observe all details of an airplane trip from the time the crew checks in an hour before flight time until the airplane is wheeled to the hangar for its regular check-up." As a result of this trip, a full page spread with pictures appeared in a prominent Schenectady newspaper.

The week before we met Jack a new ticket office had been opened in White Plains, the county seat of Westchester. Jack was asked to plan the publicity and work out the details with the other departments involved. For the opening of this office there was the traditional ribbon-cutting ceremony attended by Miss White Plains, the acting county executive, several of the top county and local officials, prominent business men, and civic leaders. Company officials and attractive stewardesses were also present. "It was somewhat like a three-ring circus," Jack recalled. "I was busy setting up pictures for the newspapers, helping to make certain our distinguished guests and members of the press were properly taken care of and then being sure to get one of our stewardesses to Radio Station WFAS in time to appear on a special program. In order to get the broadcast I first had to show the station why it was a good idea, then get together with the announcer and give him a list of suggested questions. The stewardess had to be briefed on what to say. This was of course only a small project but you can easily see how many details have to be planned ahead and carefully executed.

"We make many trips to the airport because so many famous personalities and people in the news are always arriving and departing," Jack said. "Actually we are there to assist the passenger and the press—sort of like a master of ceremonies, except that we stand in the background waiting for a cue to lend assistance as much as possible."

One of Jack's biggest projects involved planning all the details for a scientific expedition with the Hayden Planetarium to Hudson Bay to photograph the June 1954 eclipse of the sun. The eclipse flight left at midnight loaded with photographers and special photographic and other scientific equipment, and did not return until twelve hours later. This job required almost a year of advance planning. (See also Chapter 4).

Those special projects (such as described above) in which Jack participates, serve to add a touch of spice to what can be, for the most part, a routine and tiring job. Answering a constant stream of telephone calls becomes routine although individual calls are not. Most calls are of a "service nature"—requests for reservations, flight information, operating or financial statistics and historical or biographical data. Hundreds of calls that don't actually belong in public relations are received because so many people think of the public relations department as the logical place to obtain information about the company. Many calls can be answered immediately, some require minutes or hours of investigation and research. Between phone calls, writing and special assignments are accomplished but often these must wait until after five o'clock. Doing odd jobs for others is another frequent chore but none of this deters Jack Coneybear, for he says:

"I like people and I like to do things for them. That's all-important in a job like mine. There isn't a week that goes by either when I don't meet and have a chance to talk with someone important or learn something interesting which adds to my background of knowledge. A job like this is an education in itself but I would advise any young man or woman thinking of entering public relations not to skip college. Maybe it was the best thing for me, I'll never know. Certainly the many people I met helped broaden my experience and outlook, but I feel sure that a college education is important. It's foolish to put it off, for once you are out working you will find little or no time for further formal education, if you have a job that is as busy and as much fun as mine!"

CHAPTER

15

A Public Relations Department Is Born

So far we have discussed the activities of men and women connected with old, well-established public relations departments. As the closing chapter of this section we want to give you the story of James S. Haskins, public relations director of the American Oil Company, who established this organization's first public relations department in 1952. But first a little background on the company itself, and then on Jim Haskins.

Every motorist who drives through the eighteen states that stretch from Maine to Florida and inland as far as Ohio, is probably familiar with the red and white oval that encircles the letters AMOCO. This colorful oval trademark identifies the more than 10,000 modern service stations which sell gasoline, oil, tires, batteries and other products of the American Oil Company. While a majority of these service station dealers own and operate their own business, they buy their gasoline and other products from the company.

On the other hand, the American Oil Company is a medium-sized integrated oil company, with 8,500 employees. It owns and operates its own refining and production and pipeline as well as other transportation facilities. The home office is in the new AMOCO building at Fifth Avenue and 46th Street, New York City, where more than 500 employees direct the operations of the company.

And as for Jim Haskins—he is the son of a retired Michigan weekly newspaper publisher. His business experience started during grammar school days thirty-five years ago when he swept the floor, ran errands, set type, and folded papers in his father's print shop.

During college, he earned the biggest share of his expenses reporting sports for a Detroit daily newspaper, working in the college's agricultural publications department and editing the *Michigan State News*, then a semi-weekly college newspaper. Ironically, he had refused several job offers when he was an undergraduate but by the time he graduated the depression had set in and he was unable to find a small daily newspaper that could afford to hire him.

On a trip to Detroit to collect his final check for his sports writing, Mr. Haskins met a newspaper friend who sent him to see the widely-known editor and writer, the late Malcolm Bingay, of the Detroit *Free Press*. This editor hired him on the spot, assigned him to a city-desk reporting job, and three months later sent him to Saginaw, Michigan, to open the Saginaw Valley Free Press News Bureau. Here Mr. Haskins covered a wide territory and got more than his share of writing experience, usually producing four to five columns a day. Two years later he was transferred back to Detroit with the *Free Press* and a few months later accepted a better position with the Associated Press in Boston. Re-assigned to the Detroit bureau of this news service in 1936, he helped cover the famous General Motors sit-down strike early in 1937. After the strike ended he was hired back by the *Free Press* with a modest salary increase. The rest of Mr. Haskins' eleven years of newspaper experience was on the *Free Press* except for one year on the Detroit *News*.

"The thirties were pretty hectic for newspapermen, a sort of merry-go-round," Mr. Haskins recalled. "In those depression days about the only way to get a raise was to switch jobs. And I did it, too. Finally in 1942 I left the newspaper game to join the public relations agency of Carl Byoir and Associates in New York. Why did I get into public relations? Simple! I had a wife and a son and we had to eat. In those days there wasn't much money to be made reporting for a newspaper."

Mr. Haskins' four years at Carl Byoir were busy ones because in those wartime years they were short on staff and long on problems. But he now looks back to this period as being one in which he received good experience in the basic principles and techniques of public relations. His next move was to become assistant public relations director for Schenley Distillers Corporation. There, one of his first assignments was the creation of a special booklet: *Timely Tips for Veterans*, which was so timely that 100,000 were distributed on individual requests of veterans. Said the late Glenn Griswold in his September 23, 1946, *Public Relations News:*

"Occasionally a piece of public relations promotion fits a critical need so perfectly that it spreads around the country like a prairie fire. Such was the experience of the boys in the PR department of Schenley Distillers Corporation when they decided to get out a book explaining to their veteran employees how to get unused leave pay and full benefits of the National Service Life Insurance."

Mr. Haskins next moved into the petroleum industry. He was selected one of the first field representatives of the Fred Eldean Organization, Inc., a public relations agency which conceived and carried out the organization of the Oil Industry Information Committee program. Mr. Haskins spent three years as a district representative—two years in Chicago, where he helped organize the midwestern committees of the industry-wide program, and one year in charge of the New York-New Jersey district. Then when the American Petroleum Institute, the organization under which the program operated, took over actual direction of the program on January 1, 1950, Mr. Haskins was designated national field supervisor of the public relations effort, a post he held until he resigned January 1, 1952.

It was this latter assignment that brought Mr. Haskins to the attention of the American Oil Company. And when Mr. Haskins left his industry post, the president of the oil company hired him as an outside consultant to make a one-month study to determine if it was feasible for the company to start a public relations program. During this study Mr. Haskins had conferences with twenty-five company executives at various levels in several cities. To each man he explained that he had been employed as a consultant to study the public relations needs of the company and to recommend how such a program could be launched.

"If there were a public relations department in this company, what could such a department do to help you in your job?" he asked each man interviewed.

He reported back to the president that there was a general recognition of the fact that the company needed a formalized public relations program, although company men had previously carried out some very excellent public relations efforts. He found that employees in the field felt they were handicapped by lack of information to carry out effective public relations projects and that furthermore they were too busy to make such sporadic efforts continuous and thereby effective. He concluded that AMOCO was ready for a formal public relations program and recommended that it be developed slowly but soundly by a small but well-qualified staff. He reported further that the public relations program had to be geared to available company manpower and flexible enough to incorporate ideas and projects suggested by people in the field.

Impressed by the practical logic of the study and the qualifications of its author, the board of directors approved the president's recommendation that a public relations department be created by hiring Mr. Haskins and one secretary.

The program was launched formally in August, 1952, at a management conference during which the company president said it would require the co-operation of every employee to make the new program successful and that he intended to devote as much time as required to help develop the necessary management policies. Then he explained that he would expect Mr. Haskins to be responsible for (1) clearance and preparation of all company statements for release to newspapers, radio and TV stations (except purely local stories handled by division sales offices and others in the field), (2) maintenance of company contacts with trade publications, news wire services and other national media, and (3) development of an adequate public relations staff to work with everyone in the company.

It was agreed that Mr. Haskins' first assignment would be to concentrate on getting acquainted with all divisions and operations of the company. He visited the fifteen sales divisions from Maine to Florida, many of the deep-water terminals and also the refining, production and pipeline facilities in Texas. But it was not long before he found himself knee-deep in many activities that could not wait. There was the nationwide oil strike which required skillful handling of good and bad publicity, there were industry meetings to attend, important localized news releases and other jobs of getting information to people within the company. Almost overnight the newly established public relations department had become a company necessity.

"Our department's policy from the first has been to concentrate on localized news," Mr. Haskins explained. "We feel that stories about our people in their home town papers will do more good than a nationwide general release. A story about a man being promoted, transferred, retired or otherwise honored which is taken to the local paper by our local oil man is most effective.

"A good example of what I mean occurred six months after I reported for work at AMOCO. Fifty-five of our salesmen earned a seven-day trip to Texas to visit the oil fields and refinery. This provided me with the first opportunity to supply each division with a pattern story and instructions to deliver the story to the editors of the man's home town newspaper. Then I wrote a second story in Texas and mailed it direct to the same home town newspapers. I did it myself because I was afraid the division managers would think I was overburdening them. About 90 per cent of the first stories placed with the newspapers on a local basis were used, several with pictures of our local men, while only 10 per cent of my stories mailed from Texas were used. That convinced me and thereafter I made it a policy always to have the division manager place a story that had a local angle. They like it better that way too."

One thing Mr. Haskins recognized immediately was the need for improving the communications between management and employees in the field. But this is something that had to be approached carefully and gradually. Mr. Haskins availed himself of every opportunity to speak at divisional sales meetings, sales clinics, or even to individual employees about the essential and fundamental steps required to inaugurate a formal public relations program in the company.

"We had to point out that it was to the company's best interests for our men out in the field to do the talking for the company in their community," said Mr. Haskins. "We had to point out that in reality the employee in the field is 'Mr.

AMOCO' in his community. We had to remind them that all we could do was to counsel them when a problem came up in which our department had more experience than they. And gradually a two-way communication began to develop, particularly in reference to working with newspapers. We suggested that good relationships with the press are far more important than mere columns of publicity that might be printed."

One suggestion made by the department to field people was that they get acquainted with the editors in their territory by paying them a visit when they had no story to place. Another suggestion was that salesmen or others in the field should tip off the newspapers when they knew about a good human-interest story, a serious accident, or other local story—especially when it did not concern the company or the oil industry. Still another was to time their visits to newspaper offices at a time when the editors would not be working frantically on a copy deadline.

"We also had to clear up confusion between the terms of 'advertising,' 'industrial relations,' 'public relations' and 'sales promotion,'" Mr. Haskins recalled. "We insisted that there is a little of each of these in any worth-while project and we suggested we not confuse the issue by trying to claim any credit for public relations. Fortunately, such a project developed during my first year with the company to provide a good example of our public relations philosophy.

"It happened in Baltimore. Our local company people had been participating in a community-wide effort to sell 15,000 season tickets so that Baltimore could be assured of a professional football franchise. The committee performed miracles in a month's time but there still were 1,700 tickets to sell within a week of the league meeting. Our advertising manager suggested that the company offer to guarantee the last 1,700 tickets.

"At this point our department was called in to handle the publicity. A press conference was arranged in the name of the Citizens Committee chairman, who did all the talking about the project including the part our company played in it. The result was nationwide publicity and our company gained added prestige in trade circles as a result of a story in *Tide* magazine. Its headline read: 'Amoco Helps Baltimore Get a Football Franchise—Through a Smart Public Relations Coup, the Oil Company Helps the City and Nets Good Will.' After telling the essentials of our company promotional effort, *Tide* said this in the last paragraph:

" 'Reportedly, the public's delighted reaction to this public relations gesture was immediate and concrete. Drivers pulling up at Amoco service stations warmly thanked the attendants. Whether football fans or not, most Baltimoreans had a new awareness of one of its corporate citizens.'

"This was a good example of the technique of letting others tell nice things about a company instead of bragging about it yourself," Mr. Haskins concluded.

Another step in the improvement of communications in the company came eighteen months after the public relations department was born. The company's industrial relations director, aided by a sample layout and planning provided by the public relations department, convinced management that it was time to launch an employee magazine. This lusty infant, *The Amoco Oval*, sprang up full grown in December, 1953, as a sixteen-page slick-paper magazine. Its contents were carefully balanced with articles and news of AMOCO employees and it was received enthusiastically throughout the entire company. The main result of this magazine was that it provides a completely new avenue of communications between top management and employees.

By 1955 the public relations department had a head count of five. In addition to Mr. Haskins, who reports directly to the company president, there were now an exceptionally well-qualified assistant director, a writer, and two secretaries. No doubt the department will grow larger as the company it serves continues to expand. The growth will be gradual, however, because Mr. Haskins firmly believes that his department's chief function is one of counseling and guiding over-all public relations policies and activities of his company rather than trying to handle such matters centrally.

"Public relations," he insists, "is doing the right thing and then telling the community what you are doing. Therefore, our public relations program must be one of frankness, honesty, and sincerity. Any statement made by a company official or an employee to the press must accurately reflect the company's accomplishments and policies. That is why we feel our public relations is a part of the job of everyone on our company payroll."

PART 3

YOUR PUBLIC RELATIONS CAREER

CHAPTER

16

Is Public Relations For You?

You have had an opportunity to see how public relations serves in various fields and what some practitioners have accomplished. You should know that like any profession, it offers stimulation and frustration, satisfaction and discontent, as well as financial rewards to some and a mere living to others.

Still interested in the profession? Yes? Good! Then let's see what personality traits you should possess if you would seriously consider entering the field. The following are among the most important:

Enthusiasm—Enthusiasm is necessary for every job assignment. It must be sincere, contagious, and strong enough to inspire others to work with you.

Administrative Ability—You should be able to teach others how to do their job as well as direct their activities. You need executive ability to work successfully with those in your own as well as in other departments, particularly when you are called upon to participate in policy decisions.

Leadership—In addition to directing the activities of others, you must possess the type of personality that inspires and leads your associates to greater endeavor.

Fondness for People—You must like people in spite of whatever undesirable qualities they may have and you should be able to sympathize and understand why they behave and think as they do. Being a lifetime observer and student of human nature is one of the most important prerequisites for this profession.

Dependability—You must be as good as your word and the kind of person who can be depended upon to deliver the goods when promised.

Consistency—Can you be relied upon to think things through logically and to be consistent in your reasoning? At the same time will your thinking be sufficiently flexible and alert to the need for change?

Honesty—The importance of this trait goes without saying.

Perseverance—You must have the guts to stick to your job assignment through thick and thin.

Courage—Have you the courage to stick up for what you think is right and to tell someone when they are wrong? Are you also able to keep your head during an emergency or do you go to pieces? Public relations often deals with emergencies when courage and a clear head are essential.

Ability to Listen—In public relations, as in any business, it is important that you be a good listener. One way to learn what is going on about you is to keep your ears open and let the other fellow do the talking. Incidentally, good listening habits are essential for the newspaper reporter.

How many of the above qualifications do you have? Be honest, for you will fool no one but yourself. It is probably too early in life for you to judge your administrative and leadership abilities even if you have been active in school affairs and demonstrated both of these qualities. Perhaps you are the retiring type that did not care to participate in college affairs. Thus your leadership and executive abilities may be latent—ready to pop out later—but you must possess them if you hope eventually to go to the top.

We asked Dorcas Campbell (whom we met in Chapter 14) what she considered the most desirable personality traits for a young man or woman entering public relations. She listed the following:

Resourcefulness—because your day-to-day contacts and the demands made upon you are heavy and vary greatly.

Alertness—to what is going on about you. You should be continually challenged by the ever-present need for change.

Imagination—ability to see the importance of little things.

Vision—always focus on the future, for you must see today what is needed tomorrow and next year. Enthusiasm for detail and routine are essential too. Even a creative genius needs a good head for detail.

Loyalty—in word and deed to the various groups you serve.

Dependability—it is just as important to do your job assignments on time as it is to run a train on schedule.

Adaptability—to adjust quickly to any situation. Like a juggler you must be able to keep several balls in the air at the same time, skillfully adding or taking away a ball but without losing control.

Self-Control—you will need it when you are tempted to tear into some nasty character, when the telephone won't leave you alone, or when another unexpected crisis arises.

"PR Help Wanted"

We strongly urge you to read the article in the July, 1954 issue of *Public Relations Journal* entitled: "PR Help Wanted" by Robert McDevitt. It is based on the co-operative efforts of 165 public relations executives who answered a questionnaire survey and told of their experience in the field of personnel development for public relations. The article presents much useful information that will help you better to understand what qualities are considered most important by leading public relations executives.

Some of the questions which were asked include: "Which of the following subjects do you consider of most value for a career in public relations?" (twelve choices are listed). "Are extracurricular activities in college important as training for public relations work?" "If so, which do you consider to be of most value?" "What are the qualities and/or qualifications you consider important in a person applying for a public relations job?" "Where do you think the coming opportunities in public relations are?" "Where do you turn when you want new employees?" We recommend the article highly.

For Men Only

There is one drawback to many public relations assignments which you should seriously consider before you get started. Great demands may be made on your time at the expense of your personal life. A public relations man or woman, just like a doctor, is on call twenty-four hours a day, is sometimes required to work around the clock, and is often forced to travel at a moment's notice. Such demands come without regard for any personal plans you may have. They make public relations a questionable career for the man or woman who insists on living a normal life. By "normal" we mean a life within a set routine—the usual work week of five days, nine to five. Such is not the lot of many public relations people, and it may not be yours.

When you are young and not tied down with a mate or family, this is unimportant. We expect, though, that you will get married and raise a family. As you work your way up in the profession, you may well find yourself spending many nights at the office and traveling a great deal so that you will seldom be home. Many a happy marriage has reached a point of crisis because the wife found that she could not stand such a life.

If you really are resolved to make a career of public relations, this warning won't dissuade you. Nevertheless, we strongly advise that when you pop the question, you be fair to your fiancée and tell her exactly what she can expect.

A Word to the Ladies

You too may expect that your job in a public relations office will not be a settled five-day week with your hours limited to eight hours a day. There will be crises, special promotions, and a hundred unexpected events to claim your time and energy—often when you have a heavy date. If you find that the demands on your time interfere with your personal life, you have two alternatives:

1. Ask your beau to rescue you by proposing.
2. Forget the men altogether, plunge into the job, and become an honest-to-goodness career woman.

She Knew What She Wanted

"As a professor of composition once said, 'First you must have something to write about, then you can write.' I'd like to suggest a paraphrase of this observation," Mary Rose Noel told us. "First you must decide what you want to be (or do), and then be it (or do it)."

Few young people have the good fortune to know exactly what they want to do. Mary Rose Noel was an exception to this statement, for even in Chicago's Hibbard Grammar School she wanted to be a journalist. A reporter on the school paper, she continued this activity in high school where she started as a cub reporter and at graduation was literary editor, spending all her spare time working on the paper. At Northwestern University she took her degree in journalism and just before graduation was recommended for a part-time job as a helper to the publicist of an ice show. "That did it," she said. "I realized then that public relations was what I wanted. It was like being a reporter on a paper, but instead of reporting to just one paper, the publicist could cover all newspapers, radio, and TV, and could write features, news stories, interviews, etc."

When the ice show was over, so was Miss Noel's job. A week later she was assistant director of public relations for the Chicago Council—Boy Scouts of America. Three months later she was the director and remained in that position for four and a half years until asked to join American Airlines as a press representative in Chicago.

"A word of advice to the young ladies," she added. "Be proud of your sex, but don't trade on it. Maintain a friendly, ladylike attitude with all you meet and you'll keep your self-respect. You can do a man's job but don't go feminine if the hours are long and the situation gets tense. If you're working for an airline, and a special shipment is scheduled to arrive at 4:00 A.M., accept it as part of your duty to be on hand. Don't make a production out of it. You have a job to do. Do it. Pleasant working conditions include the ability to get along with people, particularly your co-workers.

"Public relations is a comparatively young profession. It has a great appeal to people who like to see ideas materialize—on paper, through pictures, in magazines, on the air. More and more industries, individuals, companies, and organizations realize the power of publicity. Women who aren't afraid to work irregular hours, who are creative, who enjoy the excitement of an unpredictable day, should be well qualified. Also, a woman can be a public relations adviser right out of her own home. All she needs is a typewriter, telephone, imagination, and the right contacts."

And Finally

Not everyone is fortunate enough to choose the right job the first time. A few lucky people know from an early age what they want to do in life and prepare themselves accordingly. If the idea of doing public relations really excites you, if you have the proper temperament for the business, if you have some aptitude for writing, if you are willing to prepare yourself for the profession and make the necessary sacrifices, then we say: "Go to it and good luck to you!"

CHAPTER

17

Preparing for Your Public Relations Career

GETTING YOUR TRAINING

Every professional man must receive his formal school training and then serve a period of apprenticeship when he applies his theoretical knowledge to the solution of everyday problems. The doctor interns for two years in a hospital, the lawyer works as a law clerk, and even the new minister serves as an assistant or at best is given charge of a relatively poor parish.

You too must receive your training in school and then serve a period of apprenticeship to gain the necessary on-the-job experience and know-how. We offer the following advice which you will note parallels that given by many of the publicists we met in the previous section.

For High School Students

Perhaps you have hitched your wagon to a public relations star and believe that public relations is the one-and-only career for you. As you have already learned, not everyone is suited temperamentally for public relations; and although it is often an advantage for a young person to know what he or she wants to do before entering college, there still is a chance that you may change your mind.

Consult your school's guidance director or your principal if you need help in choosing a college. He will probably agree with us that a college liberal arts course, with a major in English or journalism, provides the best background for the young man or woman who plans to enter public relations. Later, should you decide upon a different career, you will have acquired your basic liberal arts training and can take postgraduate work in the field of your choice.

For College Students

Consider the following suggestions, for they will help you start on the road to a public relations career:

1. Be sure to take courses in writing and journalism if such are offered. The public relations survey referred to in the last chapter showed that public relations executives considered journalism the most important course to take. Public relations, economics, social sciences, business administration, psychology, writing courses, and public speaking were also considered valuable to the aspiring publicist.

Journalism courses will teach you how to write for a newspaper. You will learn what makes a good story, what the editor must have, and what techniques are used to produce usable copy. It is only through consistent practice, however, that you can develop a facility or knack for writing that will qualify you for a reporting job. So we say—

2. Write, write, write. The way to learn to write is to write. The more you write the easier you will find it to express yourself and the quicker the right words will come. The basic tool for every public relations man and woman is the written word. Try to do some writing each day, if only for fifteen minutes. Keep a diary, write a news story about something you saw, write reviews of books you have read, write imaginary interviews with people you know, try your hand at a short story—anything—as long as you write. Many

an eager, conscientious, and otherwise promising man has failed to make the grade in public relations because he lacked ability to write simple, understandable prose.

3. Extracurricular activities were considered important by almost all of the public relations executives. Take advantage of the opportunity to participate in several undergraduate activities but don't concentrate on sports. Certainly the college paper is a must because it will give you a taste of journalism and actual experience at reporting. Dramatics, student government, social clubs, debating societies, literary clubs, etc., broaden your contacts with people and offer a variety of situations and experiences.

4. Take advantage of your summer vacations to get experience in real newspaper work. A small-town newspaper will afford a better variety of experience than most large metropolitan papers. Line up a job early in the winter lest someone beat you to it!

5. Read widely and include autobiography and biography, for they will give you an insight into men's minds and show you why they think and act as they do. Read about the newspaper business and the men who contributed to its growth. Do not, however, make the mistake of thinking that a book knowledge of newspapers and newsmen is any substitute for experience. It definitely is not!

Postgraduate Work

If your financial status is such that you do not have to go to work immediately after graduation from college, you may consider taking graduate work in public relations or journalism. Such additional training will be valuable but the lack of it will not prove detrimental to your career.

Boston University was the first to establish a separate school devoted to the teaching of public relations leading to a B.S. degree. Students may take a four-year course which includes two years of regular undergraduate studies and two years of public relations; they may enter from another college after completing freshmen and sophomore years and finish their college work in the School of Public Relations and Communications; or, they may take a graduate course leading toward a M.S. degree in Public Relations.

Many other universities and colleges offer undergraduate, extension, and postgraduate courses in public relations and/or journalism. Your college personnel office should be the best place to seek advice concerning which university would best meet your requirements if you are seeking further study and/or a degree in public relations or journalism.

If you are graduating from college and have a yen to enter public relations but have had no journalism or newspaper experience and no money to attend graduate school, you should probably get yourself a full-time job and attend a university that offers journalism and writing courses at night. Later you might find a part-time job on a newspaper and eventually work into a full-time position.

You don't have to take a course in anthropology to be a success in public relations, but listen to Dorcas Campbell's observations—they're good. She says:

"I wouldn't consider hiring a person to do publicity who couldn't write, any more than I would want a stenographer who couldn't type. What employer ever tried to teach his new stenographer typing?"

To Miss Campbell training in journalism is invaluable, but only part of the formal education required for a well-rounded public relations man. She believes that an individual should get the widest possible education because every ounce of training and knowledge gives added background for cultural judgment and decision. Even the course she once took in anthropology proved useful on the job!

"A thorough knowledge of the institution where you work

is, of course, essential and this may have to be gained after you are on the job," Miss Campbell said. "But remember that the trained individual comes to the new job with technical knowledge which enables him to roll up his sleeves and go right to work, learning the ins and outs of the business as he goes along."

GETTING YOUR START

You will have to agree that almost any path may lead to a career in public relations but in your case it will be much easier, quicker, and more satisfactory if you follow the most direct route to success.

There are two approaches to a public relations career. The first is to gain newspaper training that will give you a basic skill to market, the other is to get into a company and work your way up into the public relations department. Although we believe the first is the sounder and surer method, many people have achieved their goal through the second and circumstances might make the latter preferable in your own case.

Six Ways to Get into Public Relations

1. The most frequently recommended method is to land a job on a newspaper and get a few years of good experience in that business. There is a large turnover among reporters and you should not have a difficult time finding a job, provided you have studied journalism and worked on your college newspaper. Once you have your newspaper experience you are qualified for any number of positions in public relations that require the services of an experienced newspaper man.

2. If you are particularly anxious to do public relations work in a certain industry or company, apply initially for a job in the sales department. In this capacity you will not only

learn how to sell and how to meet and deal with people, but you will also become familiar with the company, its policies and products. As you establish a good record for yourself you can make the necessary contacts within your company or industry that will eventually enable you to switch to a public relations assignment.

3. You can contact many companies to see if they have an opening in their public relations department for a beginner. You may uncover a possibility or two but most companies prefer to take employees from within the company for beginning or junior public relations assignments rather than outsiders who have had no business experience. Surveys reveal that a large percentage of public relations men come from the newspaper field and experience in that field rates high as a prerequisite for a job in public relations.

4. If you seek a career in government public relations you can probably find an opening in the information office of some Federal or state agency. Unfortunately, private industry seldom looks with enthusiasm at young people who have received all their experience in government service. Unless you are particularly interested in government service, we would not recommend that field as the best place to gain your experience. Write to the Civil Service Commission, Washington 25, D. C. or the Civil Service Commission at your state capital for information about jobs in public relations.

5. It takes less than a year for a bright young woman to complete a secretarial course. With ability to type and take shorthand, you can immediately try to find a job in a public relations office. Publishing, you will recall, offers a good field for secretaries who have a yen to work into publicity assignments.

6. One further method is suggested by Mary Rose Noel who says: "I'd like to suggest that beginners start by affiliating themselves with a non-profit organization. They can

build up contacts which will prove invaluable to them when they're ready to branch out into some lucrative position." By "non-profit" she means charitable or welfare organizations.

As a matter of fact, if you find it impossible to locate a job in public relations right off the bat, you could accept any employment and do public relations for a civic group, community chest, American Red Cross, youth group, or other non-profit organization on a volunteer basis during your spare time to gain experience and make your contacts.

Even though you have selected the business in which you want to practice public relations, we strongly urge that you resist the natural temptation of jumping in now. Get your journalism experience and *then* tackle your company or industry for a job. We don't think you'll ever regret the decision.

Miss Dorothy Ducas, public relations director of the National Foundation for Infantile Paralysis, has this advice to give young people preparing for a public relations career. It is an excellent summary statement of everything we have said in these last two chapters:

"I would say that they should do newspaper, news magazine, or news radio work first, concentrating on learning the technical tricks and making as many friends as possible. They should not be overcome by the words '*Public Relations*' which mean many different things to many different people, but keep their sights on the goal of getting a message across in a way that will make the right impact on the people to be reached. By *right,* I mean a way that will help people to understand and approve of the organization or product which is being publicized.

"It goes without saying that a successful public relations man or woman must have a pleasing personality and therefore spend time and effort on grooming, speech, and intelligent interest in affairs above and beyond those directly connected with the job. When you come right down to it, there are no substitutes for intelligence and creative imagination. Both of these are God-given, so all an individual can do is give them full play if he happens to possess them."

IT'S UP TO YOU

The future is bright for public relations. It is a business which is fast achieving professional status and is well respected. More and more companies are recognizing the need for a good public relations program and the number of people engaged in public relations or related activities is growing every year.

There are unlimited opportunities for men and women. Although men predominate as executives and comparatively few women rise to the very top, there are those who have made good and their accomplishments should give encouragement to every would-be woman publicist. Women like those whom you met in this book, plus many others who are prominent in their field, are the exceptions that prove the rule. You too can be an exception if you have what it takes.

If you accept the challenge of making your mark in public relations, we wish you much happiness and success in your work.